for N.. Charlie & Family.

THE GOLDEN FEW

by Anthony Wells

Merry Christmas

Anthony Wells

Author

December 25th, 2001

DORRANCE PUBLISHING CO., INC.
PITTSBURGH, PENNSYLVANIA 15222

The contents of this work, including, but not limited to, the accuracy of events, people, and places depicted; opinions expressed; permission to use previously published materials included and conclusions drawn from the author-presented information; and any advice given or actions advocated are solely the responsibility of the author, who assumes all liability for said work and indemnifies the publisher against any claims stemming from publication of the work.

Dorrance Publishing Co., Inc.
701 Smithfield Street
Pittsburgh, PA 15222
Visit our website at _www.dorrancebookstore.com_

ISBN: 978-1-4349-2919-8
eISBN: 978-1-4349-2271-7

DEDICATION

This book is dedicated to the memory of Air Chief Marshal Sir Keith Park, Royal  Air Force (1892-1975), who in 1940 as the air officer commanding Eleven Group, Royal Air Force, during the Battle of Britain, arguably saved the civilized world. He may be the least recognized of the great wartime commanders of modern times.

Sir Keith Rodney Park

Marshal of the Royal Air Force Lord Tedder said of Keith Park after World War Two:

"If any man won the Battle of Britain, he did. I do not believe it is realized how much that one man with his leadership, his calm judgment, and his skill, did to save, not only this country, but the world."

Marshal of the Royal Air Force the Lord Tedder, Chief of the Air Staff, 1947

CONTENTS

Prologue

All the main characters in this story were real people—the athletes in the 1936 Olympic Games are as they were, and the details of the 1936 and 1948 Olympic Games are as accurate as the historical records permit. The author was privileged to meet Don Finlay for a two-month period at the Royal Naval Convalescent Home at Osborne House on the Isle of Wight in the autumn of 1969, when the author was recovering from severe injuries sustained as a young naval lieutenant. Don Finlay, though a retired RAF group captain, was also a patient for reasons the story explains in the last chapter. Godfrey Rampling lived to be one hundred, and the father of the distinguished actress Charlotte Rampling. Godfrey Rampling is one of the greatest heroes of British athletics, the man whose wonderful race in his leg of the four-by-four hundred-meter relay led to Britain's triumphant gold medal, beating the United States and Germany in the Berlin Stadium. His story has never been fully told. The life and times of Jesse Owens have been thoroughly researched, and his four gold medals in 1936 will stand forever as a victory for freedom, and the equality of all races. Frederick and Roland Wells are the author's grandfather and father. Frederick Wells founded and owned Coventry Gear. All the details about Coventry Gear are as they were. Roland Wells was a distinguished athlete, and knew the key participants in the 1936 Games. What occurred in Coventry on the night of November 14, 1940, is ingrained in the family history of the Wells family. In order to provide coherence and focus to the overall context of this story, the life of Jesse Birkett is in part fictitious. She represents in one person several brave women from the SOE in Northern France in the winter, spring, and summer of 1944. She does, therefore, represent a quintessentially heroic group of British women who gave their all in the name of freedom, and made sacrifices above and beyond the call of duty.

The author was privileged to be mentored as a young naval officer by the late Sir Harry Hinsley, the great World War II Bletchley Park code breaker, and character in the story. The author became familiar in fine detail of Bletchley Park and the Twenty Committee's extraordinary deception work as a result of working with Sir Harry and his colleagues on a project in the late 1960s and early 1970s, and some years before the Enigma and Ultra material ever became public knowledge. He was also the chairman of the author's Ph.D. board.

The details of the Battle of Britain are accurate to the finest detail. The author has researched the life of Air Chief Marshal Sir Keith Park at the Auckland Museum in New Zealand over a period of many years.

This story is about courage, determination, never giving up in the face of enormous challenges, and pressing ahead until final victory was achieved. The story of these extraordinary people is one that should give strength and fortitude to us all, and in the year of the Olympic Games in London, cause us all to pause and remember the achievements of these remarkable people. The book is dedicated to Sir Keith Park because, as his statue in London indicates, he provided the personal leadership, strategy, and tactics that saved Britain and the civilized world at its finest hour.

The author has been privileged to write this story in novel form. The dialogue and development of the story have been interspersed with factual data that adds authenticity to the plot. The author hopes that the reader will not only enjoy the story, but also be encouraged to read further into the history of the period and discover more about these extraordinary people.

—Anthony Wells

Chapter One
THE STADIUMS

A large stadium has different meanings, memories, and relationships for most people. The stadium location, the atmosphere, the event, one's age at the time, and the overall total experience contribute to a distinct feeling that each unique memory stores as part of our human experience. Whether we were direct participants, part of a large crowd or audience, event organizers, officials, supporters or fans of one side or another, hoping maybe that one's favorite player or athlete would do well, or perhaps one's country's team will excel, whatever our role and reason for being there, the stadium is where a lot happens.

More may also happen in a stadium than you may want.

The memories from one stadium, and one event, may vary as if you had been on a different planet. The wonderful memory of a hot summer day when your baseball team went into bat to try to clinch the game, and indeed they do—you were elated. You may remember a cold, bitter winter's day when you were huddled together at your team's critical play-off game. All does not go well. It is a climatic end, the score changes in minutes, indeed seconds, and you leave the stadium dejected, and very cold. You remember the singing of the National Anthem at the one Cup Final or Super Bowl that you have ever been to. Your all time favorite vocalist's rendition still rings in your ears all these years later. The shrill of the crowd, the powerful energy of thousands of supporters, the massive feeling of expectation, hope, and loyalty combine to create an atmosphere that cannot be replicated anywhere other than this moment in time. It is a unique experience, an eclectic event that cannot be duplicated.

The stadium may mean more to some than others, and different things for different reasons. It may be the place that you identify with, outside of home and family, where you go to enjoy and experience things that take you out of yourself, and lift your spirits in the crowd to heights that the routine, maybe humdrum, way of life can never provide. The fever pitch that may be generated at a critical point in a match, a race, an attempt on a world record, or the appearance of a great performer, has a blend of human emotion, outgoing energy, and even momentary hysteria that will never be experienced anywhere, anytime, other than right there and then, in that stadium, with all those other human beings. It is an individual and collective experience. Participation may not be an option— being there is, in itself, an experience that none of our senses, our feelings, our beliefs, our loyalties, and our hearts can deny.

The cultural experience may vary across time and space. The sheer delight, emotion, and sense of energy as a soccer crowd sings their team's song is diffi- cult not to feel. *You'll Never Walk Alone*, *Amazing Grace*, or the playing of Puccini's unfinished opera *Nostrum Dorma*, can electrify a crowd. Suddenly individuals who never sing, who may never show how they feel perhaps except in the quiet recesses of their own homes, become emboldened, almost liberated by the excitement of the moment. The sum total of all the parts, all those human spirits, become one, united in the stadium. There is joy and exhilaration, smiles, and good cheer, with waving banners, mascots, and flags.

Our first stadium is a different place than any that you will have experi- enced. It is unique.

A few blocks from this stadium an old man sits outdoors at a roadside café. He is enjoying his pipe and a cup of his favorite coffee. The local newspaper lies scattered across the table. He is alone. He will be eighty-six in a few weeks time. Other than the usual aches and pains, some arthritis in his knees, and back pain after years of toiling in the local brewery as a master brewer, he is in good shape by any reasonable standards. Life has been kind to him. Many of his boyhood friends, those whom he cherished dearly and the very few that he disdained a lit- tle, have passed on—part of life's rich pattern of change. The inevitable end came to some of his closest friends earlier than anyone would ever have wanted, carried off by tuberculosis, diphtheria, a slew of different accidents in the fields and factories, and diseases that were not called cancer, because the word cancer was unknown to most. He lost his best boyhood friend in the great influenza out- break of 1919, carrying off millions more than all those who perished in the trench warfare of the Western Front, Gallipoli, and on the high seas during the Great War. He had lost other friends in the latter, cannon fodder as he called them for the ambitious goals of his nation's leaders.

Artur's mind wandered back to the days before motor cars, before the new fangled airplanes, when his first bicycle was a wonder machine for him, a tech- nological revolution that enabled him to cycle all over the area, providing hith- erto unknown mobility. Now his old legs could no longer bike—no more rides out into the country, no visits to the hop fields that he loved, to the beer houses and cellars in the villages that he had helped sustain by his fine beer. Time had marched on, and he had to be content with a very rare ride in one of the Post Buses to his favorite village of all, and his all time favorite beer house. The gar- den in summer was a joy—music, laughter, merriment, honest people having fun and beer in what was for them their own special little heaven.

Artur's wife, Honnelore, had passed away some years before, a victim of apparent heart disease, though some said she had others things wrong with her, with swelling of her breasts and armpits. She had died in a lot of pain, and Artur was beyond distressed. The light of his life went out. She who had been his love and support had gone. Childless and with his faithful shepherd dog suffering from degenerative bone disease, Artur sold their small family home on the outskirts of town and moved to a one bedroom, ground floor apartment or flat where he could be close to the shops and people who knew him well, and cared about him. One of his nieces came in twice a week and cleaned house and prepared meals for him, and his church provided support. His main joy was to take his walking stick and walk to the coffee shop and meet his friends to catch up on the local news.

Today seemed to be no different. His short walk to the churchyard to lay some pretty flowers at Honnelore's graveside had been his exercise for the day. Amadeus, his dog, could scarcely make the short walk. Artur encouraged him, and together they made it there and back. Artur looked at the faithful Amadeus, and realized that time was no longer on either of their sides. A dog's life and a man's life both came together in a bond of finite reality—they looked at each other with mutual sympathy. If Amadeus could talk, he would have told Artur how much he loved him and thank him for the almost twenty wonderful years of being close to his master and his master's bride, for the care and attention they had given him, for the fun and sheer joy of the local countryside, the pleasures of canine activity, and the senses of this world—smell, the breeze, the rain and snow, the bright glorious warmth of summer, a scamper in the damp melancholy of autumnal days, the noises of the woods, and the joy of racing down bluebell laden tracks and peaty, earthy byways in the early spring. Today Amadeus and Artur were one—they shared a common bond—Artur loved his best friend, named after his favorite composer, Mozart. Artur had decided when he first acquired the shepherd puppy that he did not quite like the first name, Wolfgang. It sounded too hard, too guttural, and did not have the distinctive ring of Amadeus, with its combination of Deus, the God, and love in one name. Artur loved to slowly say his name, rolling it off his tongue in several syllables—Am-a-de-us. When they were sometimes parted in the woods he would call out Amadeus' name, with a shrill voice that had a magic tone for his loyal and devoted dog.

Today there were other noises competing with the ambient, friendly noises of the street and passersby outside the café. Amadeus was disturbed. Despite his age, Artur's companion still had his hearing—the noises were not friendly, they were not the pleasant, natural noises that made his ears prick up, and made his nose rise in the air to catch any associated smells that would accompany the noise. The noise was shrill, harsh, hard on the ears, and resounding.

Artur mumbled some words to Amadeus, soothing him, and patting him on his back, telling him not to worry. The dog's face gave all away. Amadeus could not be consoled by gentle petting. The noise disturbed him. He was fretful. The noise level rose and the dog visibly stiffened, as if coming to attention, and then did something that Amadeus only did when he was protective of his master—he growled.

The stadium was three short blocks from the café. It was a large, forbidding structure, a poor replica of a Greek or Roman amphitheater, an imitation that did not meet the connoisseur's sense and image of architectural grandeur. This was not the grandeur that was Rome, or the glory that was Greece. This structure was eldritch and macabre, an embodiment of other ideas and aspirations than those that had led several thousand years of Greek and Roman culture.

The noise reached fever pitch. Artur began to tear. His eyes were moist and he raised his right index finger to his right upper cheek to remove the small droplets. He stiffened. He was becoming angry. The noise would not abate. He could hear, feel, and sense the intensity of the event, and he became morose with a sense of foreboding that only a man of eighty-six, at this time, in this place, could truly know.

The final marching song ended, and Artur's body relaxed; Amadeus became calm, his tail lying still on the sidewalk, and he drank some water from the small bowl that Artur always obtained from the café's proprietor. The latter emerged from inside and asked Artur if he would like another coffee. Artur graciously accepted. No sooner had the words left his mouth than another noise echoed from the stadium. It was a single voice—harsh, dogmatic, full of thunder, and staccato in tenor, and the deliverance was measured, controlled, almost messianic. For Artur this was far worse than the singing and the marching music. The words sent him into an internal spasm of pent up disdain, of intolerance for the demagogic slogans and valueless rhetoric. His heart sank, and his faithful companion closed his eyes and rested his head on his master's foot, seeking solace from the blaring noise of the man's voice amplified by the stadium's massive loud speakers.

Artur's mind wandered. He could not believe that this was happening. He could not believe what he was hearing, that this was actually happening, here in his beloved city of his birth, within the country that he loved.

The rally inside the Nuremburg Stadium reached fever pitch.

The voice of the speaker was followed by a powerful chanting, a demagogic outpouring of nationalistic fervor. Then came the final incantations, the Horst Wessel song, and the singing of *Deutschland, Deutschland, und Deutschland Über Alles.*

The Nazi rally came to an end in a wave of hysteria.

Artur's body relaxed, and both he and Amadeus fell into a doze, as if the adrenalin of the stadium had evaporated, and now all was calm, all was quiet, and they could be at peace with themselves, with the world they loved.

Chapter Two
THIS IS NOT ATHENS

The Athenian gods were given homage several thousand years later by one of the great memorials of modern times—the Olympic Games. The Olympiad represents in true Greek style the challenge of the greatest athletic event that the world can produce. The outpouring of competition, hope, aspiration, and years of endless training and endeavor, is matched by the lofty goal of a common bond—people united by sport, though separated by language, creed, color, and national aspirations. It is a great coming together, when the world shows that it can rise above the clamor of political differences, conflict, and rivalry of a different kind, and values that may be juxtaposed against the lofty ideals of athletic competition.

Different cultures reflect different attitudes, different goals, and a wide range of moral, as well as pragmatic approaches to the role of sport. For some it is an individual challenge, or a team activity—a representation of the best of the best in the attempt to rise to the occasion of athletic endeavor. For some, it is about character—individual, local, and national. For the educationist, sport may be a defining goal, a means to an end—the creation of a wholesome person through sporting effort and the challenge of the field, the track, the pitch, and the rowing grew, moving in perfect harmony in the grueling race to the finish, and the sheer splendor of the individual athlete that excels, who rises above all expectations, who goes literally and metaphorically the extra mile, and conquers their own self-doubts and fears of failure to accomplish something of which they had only dreamed.

For the great Headmaster of Rugby School, Thomas Arnold, sport was about character—moral and physical courage, commitment, teamwork, togetherness, hard work, challenge, and understanding defeat and victory. For him, it was better that his young men experience victory and defeat rather than never experience either. Better to have tried and failed than never tried at all. Play hard and play fair were values to be imbued by hard experience, to be nurtured and retained. Be generous in victory, and noble in defeat. It is about the playing of the game, not the outcome. Never give up, and never surrender to self-doubt or fear. Fear of failure can be the biggest challenge. Overcoming this is, in itself, a great victory. These are values that sustained a nation, and were imbued in the national consciousness of a people who would face a different kind of challenge.

The Olympic ideal is like many things within the human experience. Ideals have to be sustained. Sometimes they can be challenged, undermined, and eroded.

While one stadium in southern Germany was concluding a rally of disproportionate implications for the world than the historic city of Nuremburg would imply, another city to the north was readying itself for another form of national outpouring that would envelop the civilized world.

The Brandenburg Gate and the Reichstag symbolized, at this moment in time, the entrance of a new culture, the likes of which the world had never seen before. It was a time of international chaos. Into this chaos now came a formidable challenge to a few, frenzied and climatic years of dramatic change. The challenge was the ideals, aspirations, camaraderie, and sense of oneness inherent in athletic endeavor and competition, where only one would win, and where coming second, or third, is good, but for some, perhaps not quite good enough. The Olympic ideal was now transposed for a few weeks—a few brief, critical, unforgettable moments in time to Berlin, Germany, and the year was 1936— a year that would see change, the likes of which the world had never seen before and hopefully will never see again.

The clash of idealism of one world was about to collide with the idealistic fanaticism of another.

To the tumultuous crowd standing in the stadium, or relaxing in the more rarefied atmosphere of private boxes, or those who may be part of the international milieu of politicians, diplomats, sports commentators and reporters, and Olympic organizers, there may be little or no sense of what transpired in the locker rooms deep beneath the stadium bleachers.

Today was not just a day at the 1936 Olympics. It was a very special day.

As the athletes arrive they want the anonymity of the secure entrance, a place where they can be protected from the crowds, the noise, the passion of international competition, and the cameras and reporters, those who want to capture celluloid images of Olympian athletes. The corridor to the locker room is a safe haven, a final separation from the noise, the bands, the heat, and the pressure. To win, or not to win, that is the question. Success, or failure, joy or disappointment, supreme victory or dismal defeat, are all now possible. In the minds and bodies of those who tread the last few precious steps from public glare to privacy, quiet, and a brief respite before the inevitable challenge before the stadium throng and international radio and press audience, are many thoughts, feelings, fears, hopes, and prayers.

The locker room door is shut.

The guards protect the athletes not just because they are the best of the best in their athletic endeavors, but also because they are the representatives of those who now seek to compete against, not just the very best of their country, but those who are proclaimed to epitomize their race, ideology, newfound way of life, and political aspirations. This is not any locker room, this is not just any Olympic gathering, just any meeting of athletes engaged in the most historic of human endeavor—athletic competition, this is about the rise of a new and formidable power in the world, and a challenge to the world order. This stadium is not a stage for the outpouring of the most neutral of all international rivalries— athletic competition. This stadium, here in Berlin, in 1936, is about to become an explosive force the likes of which the world has never experienced.

Chapter Three
THE LOCKER ROOM - BERLIN, 1936

"Welcome, good to see you. Heard a lot about you. How are you finding things?"

The hand was proffered. It was met with a firm, and friendly greeting.

"You know, I was really concerned about coming here. There was a lot of talk back home. I think you know what I mean. How these folks here are going to react to me. What their press are saying. All the talk by their leader. He is definitely different. Not quite our FDR. It's been a struggle—the boat ride, the train ride to Berlin, all the hoopla, our Embassy crowd, and these darn German photographers all dressed up in their weird outfits."

"It's a very great pleasure to meet you. I have read so much about you. Our press thinks the world of you—where I come from, we get the *Movie Tone News*; it's great to see your meets across the pond."

"Oh, it's not exactly a big deal, as we say. I'm just me. I love running. It's my life. It's what I am. It's me. I love every minute of every day when I am out there, rain or shine. The track, for me, is where I belong."

"Well, you certainly make the rest of us feel like we need to buck up, and get on with serious training. I'm a firm believer that if you want to be good, really excel and not just be the gentleman amateur we all think we are, you have to pull out all the stops, and you have to go the extra mile, so to speak."

Both grinned. The extra mile—or maybe something more, or something less.

"I saw the program, your heat's before ours."

"You're in the relay?"

"Yes."

"They've got the 100-meter heats just when all their figureheads are here. I think our ambassador is going to be watching, and a whole bunch of American reporters. Who needs that kind of audience?"

"Piece of cake! You'll walk it. Sorry, not quite the right phrase. We Brits have some odd expressions."

"I know, I'm rapidly finding out."

"I should have said that you'll sprint to the finish in fine style. How about that for a good old British compromise?"

The American athlete laughed.

As the two of them changed and prepared themselves for their races, they rubbed shoulders unknowingly. The lockers were Spartan, basic in all essentials, and contained no towels, soap, or robes.

The locker room was becoming noisier as more and more of the athletes shared personal details and greetings. The American and the Brit had set a trend. It was catching. Soon there were mutual introductions, and the dialogue flowed.

The German attendants stood at the end of the locker room aisles, almost to attention—motionless, stark faces, unsmiling, and not offering any semblance of service. One of them seemed to be more senior, a coordinator of sorts, with a lot of extra emblems on his uniform, and a marking that seemed ominous and out of place in an Olympic locker room. The swastika emblem had a peculiar feel to it—not a calming influence before an important race.

The American athlete started to massage his legs, drawing his hands along the muscles of his lower legs and then upwards to the quads and under to the hamstrings. He stretched his torso and arms in rhythmical movements, and then did a series of bends, flexing at the waist, placing the flat of his hands on the floor, with a slight bending of the knees. He then swayed at the hips, from side to side, holding his hands on his hips, reversing the direction every few gyrations.

After ten or so minutes of movement the American ceased, and ended with a series of head rotations, gently moving his head from side to side with his hands on his hips. The Brit noticed his controlled breathing—his inhalations and exhalations in perfect harmony, with his diaphragm rising and falling as his lungs expanded and collapse with each breath.

"Let me introduce you to the rest of the team. We relay types have to stick together. It's the nature of the baton! One drop, we all drop. You fellows are on your own, no one to worry about, no one to let down except yourself, of course. Come over here, chaps. I want to introduce you to the finest American athlete of all time."

Soon the relay runners were huddled together by the two adjacent lockers of the American and British athletes.

There was no lack of banter.

"What time's your race?"

"Who worries you the most?"

"What do you think about that nasty little man with the mustache who's promised to turn up, and honor us with his presence for the finals?"

"Personally, I think the man's nuts."

"Nuts isn't quite on the mark, old boy; the bastard's going to take us all down the path to war."

"Let's get off that topic, if you don't mind," said the British relay captain. "We're here to run, not take on this Nazi crowd."

"If you don't mind me asking," said a rather young and immature looking British relay runner, "how do you feel about all the ballyhoo in their press about you, you know, all that propaganda baloney about your…well, you know, you know what I mean."

"Hey, enough of that," said the American athlete's locker neighbor, "I am sure our good friend here has had quite enough of their nonsense. Let's forget that. Not quite fair."

Not quite fair.

The American looked his newfound British friend dead in the eyes and said, "Where I come from, nothing is ever fair, believe you me. I'm lucky; I can run like the wind."

"I didn't mean to insult you," said the Brit squeamishly.

"That's okay," said the American. "I know what you meant."

"Have you met everyone?"

"You know, I don't think I know all your names."

"Well, let me make a few introductions. Jesse, meet our four-by-four hundred-meter relay team."

Jesse Owens held out his hand. It was firm, positive, and a grip that resonated friendship and trust.

"This is Freddie Wolff."

"Great to meet you—I saw you during your warm up earlier. You move, man…seriously move."

Godfrey Rampling then introduced the other two members of the British four hundred-meter relay team.

"This is Bill, Bill Roberts, and this is Godfrey Brown."

There were warm handshakes, smiles, and greetings that were reminiscent of any British or American athletic club where the bond is the track, the competition, and the sound of the gun that fires the athletes into action.

"I hope you guys don't mind me saying this," Jesse hesitated, almost bit his tongue, and then went on, "oh, heck, you Brits are so different, good sports; is it really true what our coaches say, that you really do this just for the hell of running and having a good time? You're not maniacal competitors like this Nazi crowd that we are all watching?"

Godfrey Rampling was the first to respond. "You mean enthusiastic amateurs and all that—play hard, play fair, and play to win…?

"You bet you," Owens responded, "you like to win, but it's not the be all and end all, something like that."

Freddie Wolff slipped in a comment that made them all laugh, "You know, Jesse, we shouldn't really tell you this, but none of us four like all the baton passing practices, we just like to get out there and have a go. Heck, if we can't hand over a piece of wood on the move, well, we all ought to be playing bowls or something."

"I like that," Jesse Owens quipped. "I'm in the four-by-one hundred-meter relay team besides the three personal events that I'm in, and our coach pushes us hard on the changeover—we just have to practice that baton pass!"

"I saw the program; you're in the other events that we've been reading about you in the papers in the UK, "Bill Roberts added.

"I know you're in the one hundred- and two hundred-meter sprints; what's the other one, fellas? I've forgotten Jesse's other key event."

"The long jump," Godfrey Brown added without hesitation. "I saw the early pictures of you when you were still at college in the States. Ohio, I think."

"You have it, Godfrey. Right on the ball, man," said Jesse with a relaxed, almost familial tone as if he had known the four of them forever.

"I followed your progress during and after the LA Games," said the American athlete. "We are going to have quite a tussle with you guys."

As the cheerful banter continued, a fifth British athlete had been listening unobtrusively to the lively conversation. He was putting on his warm-up track suit preparatory to a training session. He was tall, handsome, with a fine bearing, and air of modest, but nonetheless unmistakable command about him.

He strolled the few feet across the locker room and said to the British relay foursome, "Well, I see you keep good company, the best of the best. Hi, we've never met; I missed meeting you in LA in '32."

A firm and friendly hand was outstretched.

Jesse Owens smiled; he felt that he would like this person. He looked Jesse straight in the eye, there was no equivocation, no hesitancy, no compromise, no polite soft handshake with the black athlete; he was genuine.

"My name is Finlay, Don Finlay."

"It's a great pleasure to meet you, Don. What event are you in, if you don't mind me asking?"

"One hundred- and ten-meter hurdles, " said Finlay, "but like you, short and sharp, and to the point, no long drawn out event for me, all over pretty quickly. I love to watch the newsreels of you in the one hundred meters."

"Well, thanks, Don. It's what I love. My old high school and college coaches made sure that I found my stride, so to speak, and I've never looked back—it doesn't pay to look back, and, hopefully, you don't see too many backs in front!"

They all burst into unanimous laughter.

"You like those jumps then, Don; just go like the wind over them suckers, hey."

Finlay was modest and gracious. "I found my form when I was an apprentice in training, and I've stuck with it ever since."

"Apprentice, what kind of apprentice were you?" asked Owens.

"I was an aircraft apprentice at a place called Halton in England. It's where the Royal Air Force trains it's technical types—what I think you Americans call enlisted technicians."

"So, are you still in the Air Force?"

"Yes, I certainly am. I got very lucky—I became a pilot, was commissioned, and am now flying the latest British fighter aircraft, just to keep me out of mischief, and in between keeping fit for hurdling."

"Well, God bless you, man; we are all going to need you if the crowd out there turns out to be as bad as some say back in the States."

Rampling interjected, "You have it right there, Jesse, we are all going to get dragged in some way or another," with a slight seriousness to his voice. "I'm like Don, except I wear brown, not light blue. Army, I'm in the British Army."

Rampling said no more. There was a modesty about him that Owens picked up on, and said no more other than to add, "Well, you are all over here, and we are over there, and somehow I think we are all going to need each other."

The subject changed.

"Well, fellas, let's go practice a little relaying, just to ensure our American cousins don't think that we are too amateurish."

Jesse Owens laughed.

The black athlete looked at them as they left for the track, and then turned to Don Finlay, "Don, I hope that you have a great race, and I hope that you and I can chat some more. We don't have to let all this competitive stuff get in the way of friendship. Your Harold Abrahams and that great Scots fella, Eric Liddell, are my all time heroes—true sportsmen. I still look at that newsreel of Abrahams in Paris in 1924, and say to myself, *I want to run like that, but also maybe little faster!*" He smiled a knowing smile.

"Jesse, can I call you Jesse?" Finlay said.

"Of course," retorted Owens.

"I think that you will do something very special, and I hope and pray for you that you show these Nazis what true sport is. They are looking to try to show us all that we are the second best; they're the number ones in everything that counts in these games. That little mustached leader of theirs thinks that people like you and me are second best, we cannot match them. Their papers are full of all this Aryan nonsense about the master race and how the rest of us are a bunch of total nonentities. We have to show them what we can do."

"Don, spoken the way I feel." Owens paused for just a few seconds, collected his thoughts and became a little introverted, quiet, and reflective. "Hitler thinks we black folk are second class, I've heard some really bad things that he's said about me and the other American black athletes. I plan to stick it to him and all his Nazi friends. Teach them that color is not what counts, but who you are, and what you do, and how you do it."

Both Finlay and Owens looked around and saw the sullen looks of the Nazi officials and attendants at the other end of the locker room area.

"Let's go practice, Don; let's show 'em what we're made of."

Owens' coach appeared as they were leaving the locker room and heading toward the covered walkway that led onto the Berlin Olympic tracks. He had a clipboard and stopwatch, and hustled Owens toward the stadium outside. Finlay paused, waited until he had left, grabbed a towel from his bag, and headed off, his mind thinking not of the practice hurdle drills that lay ahead outside, but of what Jesse Owens had said.

By God, he thought to himself, *we cannot let these people put us down; we cannot let them think that we cannot compete against them, otherwise we are finished. They will walk all over us.*

Finlay entered the stadium, and several hundred yards to the right he could see Jesse Owens limbering up, his legs rising up at a high rate, stretches to his toes, back exercises, rotational left and right stretches with his arms to the sides, and then stomach curls that made him look what he was—a truly great athlete, a lean machine, with energy that was bursting to show his form.

Finlay headed to where the British team was gathered, and looked to find the hurdles coach.

This was the beginning of a significant day, a day when athletics would never again be quite the same. When the undertones of race and color were there, when nationalism was becoming a hallmark of these games, when sporting rivalry had dimensions that went beyond reaching the tape, and when personal dignity and integrity were at stake.

The training sessions began.

In the middle of the field, the German team was marshaled like a well oiled military parade. The megaphone of the Nazi senior coach sounded forth. It was more like a call to arms, and, in a prophetic way, it was simply just that—the German leadership was sending a message, and it was unequivocal in its content.

Chapter Four
A MOMENT IN TIME

The gun fired. It was as if the air was stilled for a split second. The only sound was the starter's pistol echoing around the Berlin Stadium. The stadium froze as the flash of the gun momentarily was ahead of the noise for those farthest from the starting line. In a few brief seconds, history was made.

Don Finlay held his breath. Godfrey Rampling and his relay team were transfixed. Their bodies tensed as the man they had come to know just days before now held the world's attention. James Cleveland Owens, Jesse to his new found British friends, lifted from the start like greased lighting. His promise to Finlay was made true. As he hurtled down the 100-meter track, he never saw anyone's back. The gold medal was his, and the non-Germans in the stadium stood and roared their approval, with applause that enveloped the sports correspondents using their new fangled microphones, uttering those famous words across the air waves:

"It's Owens; it's Jesse Owens, and he's won the gold, the new one hundred-meter Olympic champion is from the United States. He's left them all behind. He's done it!"

The five British athletes cheered until their voices were hoarse. August 3, 1936, was a moment in time. One hundred and ten thousand people on that August day in 1936 were enraptured by his achievement—his athleticism, his physique and power, his natural grace, and his sportsmanship in victory—shaking hands and smiling with those against whom he had competed—and his modesty in winning the greatest accolades of all. This was no blonde Aryan, no Nazi propaganda icon to be revered by the Nazi propaganda machine. This was a black American from the heartland of the United States. He had defied the odds, the racist demagogy of the Third Reich, and come through to win above and beyond the much vaunted predictions of Hitler's media controllers.

On August 4, Jesse Owens went on to win gold in the long jump, the 200-meter gold medal on August 5, and his crowning glory came in the 4-by-100-meter relay team event on August 9 by winning his fourth gold medal in the Berlin Olympics. He passed, not only into the history books, he also created in those six magical days a benchmark for international sportsmanship that was unrivaled, and in the face of a political regime that had set its goal on demonstrating Aryan mastery. In those four momentous events, Jesse Owens destroyed Nazi dogma.

Don Finlay and Godfrey Rampling entered the locker room. Jesse appeared from the showers. His smile was the smile of a man who recognized true new-found friends.

Chapter Five
COVENTRY AIRPORT, ENGLAND

The teenage boy waved the batons, directing the tail dragger to its parking place. It was a way he could make some money during the school holidays—money was short at home, and doing odd jobs at the airport was something that he enjoyed. Jim Stirling never took his eye off the little de Havilland Moth as it landed and taxied over to the ramp area.

Inside the tight cockpit was one of his all-time favorite people—a young man hidden by his goggles and leather flying helmet, smiling from his open cockpit on a blustery day that created a challenge to landing the light bi-plane. Roland Wells gave him a big smile as he taxied within hailing distance. Jim ushered the Moth into its tie-down position, crossed the batons to indicate that he was to stop and hold the brakes, while Roland cut the engine. The propeller stopped and Jim dutifully placed the chocks against the main gear tires and then scrambled back along the fuselage to secure the tail wheel.

"How you doing, Jim, had a few good days since I left the other day? The weather's been kind—I had no problem with the ride back from Oxford."

"It's been quiet, sir; not much flying going on and I kept busy washing several of the trainers. We did have some excitement today. And by the way, your father is here, he's been here for a few hours. There's also a message for you in the crew room. I think it's from the factory. A Miss Jesse called you several times. My boss has the message for you."

"So what is the excitement all about?" Roland had undone his harness, climbed out of the cockpit, took his goggles and leather helmet off, and undid the zippers on his leather fleeced flying boots.

"There is a special plane here—the people inside said it was a fighter—called it a prototype or something like that."

"Does it have markings? You know, like the RAF roundels on the side?"

"No. It's in like a camouflage color—quite different from anything we've ever had at the field before—looks great! Terrific-looking engine and the cockpit is fantastic. I chocked it when it landed. While the pilot was inside with all the other people that turned up, I climbed up and looked inside—wow, what a sight…then, a man came running out and told me to get down and don't come back until I was told!"

"Okay. I wonder what that was all about."

"Well, your father can tell you…he's in there with a whole lot of other very important people, including a couple of men in RAF uniforms—bit like what you wear, but they had a lot more stripes on their sleeves—much older than you…looked really senior."

"Well, well. Let's go inside. Can you refuel her please, Jim, when you've finished your other jobs."

"I can do that now, sir; I've nothing else to do. I'll go get the fuel truck right now. When are you flying next?"

"Tomorrow, if I have my way…down to Dover, and then a boat, and then a train to Berlin."

"Berlin…where's that? Isn't that Germany, or somewhere?"

"It's Germany alright, Jim. The Olympic Games…that's where I'm heading, if my father says yes."

"Olympic Games…it's been in all the papers…quite a show…lot of great runners."

"You've got the idea. I'm off to see some of my friends pick up some medals, hopefully. Okay, Jim, let's get her topped up please. I'll see you inside when you're done. By the way, where is the mystery airplane now? Did it vanish into thin air?"

"Gosh, no, sir! After my little 'argy-bargy' with the stiff upper lip gent, it was towed over to the far hangar, you know, the one that the folks from Rolls and your father's other people use. I'm not allowed near it. There's a guard on duty. The hangar doors are closed."

"Well, well, that is one for the books…I wonder what's afoot," said Roland, and gave a thumbs up to Jim as he departed.

Jim left to get the fuel truck.

Roland went to the pilot's ready room where he could change. He took a suit out of his bag and some smart-looking black Oxford brogues to match his dark pinstripe suit. The white shirt was crumpled and he thought to himself that his mother would not be happy if she saw the state of it. He adjusted a dark blue matching tie that he put on while examining his attire in the ancient mirror that had long ago lost its luster. He made a mental note to ask Jim to polish the mirror.

Roland entered the airport private lounge area, reserved for VIPs and airplane owners.

He was suddenly, instantaneously taken aback. His father, Frederick Wells, was sitting between two RAF officers, an air vice marshal and a group captain, the latter sporting a rather effete mustache that looked as if it received serious grooming. Around them sat a gaggle of luminaries that Roland recognized, but with whom he could not claim any form of familiarity. They were his father's closest held friends and colleagues in the aviation industry. The conversation was intense. The subject was self evident—the aircraft that Jim had described.

"It's not only our future, it's our only hope if the Huns go the way Winston and his supporters predict," said the air vice marshal in a voice that was not just deadly serious, it had a ring of prophetic righteousness. "I just hope that we can build enough in time and then I hope that we can train enough good pilots to fly them. We are behind the curve in almost every domain. We have to get into gear now. And, speaking of gears, how are things with your systems, sir?" Air Vice Marshal Keith Park said to Frederick Wells in his fine New Zealand accent.

"Keith, we're on the ball, day and night, at Coventry Gear. That's not the problem. The engine is not the problem. The Merlin is Rolls' greatest achievement to date—it's a winner. The problem is that R.J. came up with the greatest design of all time, God bless him, but only just in time. The problem is can we in industry give you the production numbers before things go south? The Air Ministry is going to have to place orders now, and we will have to ramp up as if there is no tomorrow, because, believe you me, the ME109 is no spring chicken; it's a deadly machine that will lick what we have in the skies at present. Do you agree, gentlemen?" As he turned, he faced a nodding audience.

"Freddie, you are one hundred per cent correct," said the chief engineer from Rolls Royce, followed by Vickers Supermarine's chief test pilot, who had flown the airplane into Coventry and responded, "I'm too old to do it again in the next shootout, but I can tell all of you gentlemen, right now, if we don't have this aircraft in production in the hundreds by years-end, we will find that by 1939, at the latest, we will be naked in the air with no serious credible fighter defense."

Air Vice Marshal Keith Park walked around the room—he paused, looked everyone individually in the eye, and said quite unequivocally, "The message is simple and clear, I will report to the AOC immediately, and I am sure he will call the air minister. Air Chief Marshal Dowding is no slouch when it comes to telling Whitehall what we need and why. He'll go to the mat over this one. Leave it to me. Alright, we'd better head back to London." He turned and saw Roland standing just inside the doorway. "And whose company do we have the pleasure of?"

"Wells, sir, Roland Wells; I'm Mr. Wells' son. I'm also Pilot Officer Wells, Royal Air Force Volunteer Reserve, in my spare time. Just finished basic flying training in a Tiger Moth, a step up from the Moth that I've just flown in from training in Oxford. My dad owns the Moth."

"But, you fly it?" inquired Park, "Right?"

"Yes, sir."

"I have the picture. We're going to need you young Wells, and all your best friends who fly, and it won't be in de Havilland Moths!"

"I'm ready, sir."

The party spent several minutes in final discussions about schedule, the next meeting in London at the Air Ministry, and a flight demonstration at RAF Station Biggin Hill. The industry delegation escorted Park and his chief of staff out of the airport to their taxi that would take them both to Coventry Station.

Frederick Wells reappeared and told his son that they needed to chat, head for his car, and drive to the factory in Coventry. Roland questioned that wasn't it dinnertime, and wouldn't Mother be wondering where they both were for dinner? Frederick said that he had made a call to home. They would be home by about nine o'clock. They had a lot to do, and the team from Rolls Royce would be coming back with them to the factory.

Roland did not dare ask his father the whys and wherefores in front of the other men—not appropriate. His father made one brief comment, "In the car...I'll fill you in."

The ride into Coventry Gear was tense. Roland's father spelled out the facts—the plane hidden out of sight in the hangar was the prototype Spitfire, his great friend R. J. Mitchell's design come true, his legacy to Britain before he died, and as far as Frederick Wells was concerned, Britain's and the Royal Air Force's only hope with another aircraft that his father also clearly loved called the Hurricane, made by Hawker to save Britain's air defenses in the likelihood of war. Roland had heard his father say countless times over the last few years that war with Germany, the Third Reich as Adolph Hitler called it, was inevitable. "Mr. Churchill," he would say, "has it right, and as for the Chamberlain crowd and all their fellow travelers, well, they will be cast aside once the going gets tough."

Frederick Wells spent the next four hours going over a lot of engineering detail with the men from Rolls Royce and his own design and management team. Roland was a fly on the wall. As the youngest and least experienced person present, he simply kept quiet. He never uttered a word, except to excuse himself to make a phone call. He was late calling his girlfriend, Jesse Birkett. She understood. He confided in her his biggest fear—what would be his father's reaction when he told him he was off to Berlin first thing in the morning...to the Olympic Games, when his father clearly was enmeshed in a myriad of problems at the factory.

"It's simple," she said, "convince him that the only reason that you are going is to show the Nazis that the British team has not only supporters, but that Britain is made of sterner stuff than all their people dressed up in those hideous black uniforms. Oh, and by the way, whatever you say, do not mention that you are really going to cheer on your friends. He knows that you are very disappointed just missing the team...he's very proud of you, but make it sound like this is for 'King and Country,' not a good time with the boys...you know what I mean, Roland. He will appreciate the loyalty bit, the sheer patriotism."

"Jesse, you are terrible," Roland paused, "but you are right...my dad hates those Nazis with a vengeance. I know he's hoping that we stick it to them. His worst fear is that they win all, take the medals, and Hitler and his master race gang crow over the rest of the world, particularly the British."

"Tell him that you want to be there to debunk all that Aryan nonsense, all that racist goggled goop. He'll say yes, trust me."

"You're right. I think it'll work."

"Just one other tiny little piece of advice—don't, whatever you do, mention your friend Don Finlay, otherwise he will smell a rat and then he'll have visions of you and your RAF cronies drinking in some Berlin beer garden, and it's really all about a good time."

Jesse then added, "By the way, do you know that your dad has got a lot of things going on out at the field with his friends from London—the RAF and people from the Air Ministry. While you've been off doing your flying training in Oxford, they've opened up and now sealed a whole hangar out there. Some trucks arrived with containers. Everything is locked away in secure rooms. And, well this is the interesting part; your dad said to me that he thinks he can use my German language skills to help him and some other people. He said no more than this. I told him my French was better. He said not to worry, my German is good enough. So what is going on, I wonder?"

"I have no idea. Let me find out when I talk with my dad."

"Just don't mention your running friends, whatever you do. He's very intense right now. At the factory, he is totally immersed in some things."

"Got it." Roland spread verbal felicitations across the telephone wires and said a romantic goodnight.

Jesse reminded him that if he took off in the morning, to be careful, watch the weather, and don't run out of fuel…she was persistent. Roland got the message. He said one word, "Roger."

Chapter Six
WILL BERLIN BECKON?

Frederick Wells was never an easy sell. He worked hard, and all around him did the same. He was a totally self-made man. He was a West Country man, born and bred in Westbury on the outskirts of Wells, Somerset, the site of one of England's majestic cathedrals, a far cry from the throbbing industrial denizens of Coventry and the English Midlands. He taught himself advanced engineering before the British universities offered engineering degrees. He conceived uniquely the techniques and technologies to meet the growing post World War I demand for precision gears for what was to become the burgeoning British aircraft industry. He was a visionary with a one-of-a-kind technical gift with all the business acumen and skills to build the finest precision gear company in the UK, Coventry Gear. In addition, he figured out that the production secret for his business were the machine tools that could cut intricately the gears that he personally designed, gears that would enable Britain to build some of the finest products for its time.

What Frederick Wells did not know, but rapidly became to foresee, was that Coventry Gear had the technical solution to several key systems that would harness the equally great engineering and design genius of people like R. J. Mitchell, the brilliant designer of the Vickers Supermarine Spitfire, whose predecessor had won the Schneider Trophy. As the 1920s progressed through the Great Depression into the 1930s, Frederick Wells had created a unique engineering capability, indeed a national asset. Coventry Gear was now a jewel in the crown of the defense aviation industry. By the time of the 1936 Olympic Games and the massive rearmament programs underway in Nazi Germany, he could see that he now had not just a major business responsibility, but also a patriotic national duty to make several critical things happen.

Freddie Wells was no walk over, and his son now had to confront his father that he needed to leave for Berlin just when things were heating up in Coventry and the Air Ministry in London.

"Come on in, Roland; you don't have to knock, you know that."

"Dad, can we chat please?"

"Of course, pull up a chair."

"What's up?" his father said in a relax manner. "You didn't bend the Moth, did you?" he said with a sage look on his face and a grin that said, "I am not serious."

"No, Dad, it's not the plane. It's the Olympics. I would like to fly to Dover, take the boat and train, and arrive in Berlin in time to support several crucial British events—races that I would dearly love to witness and cheer on our people. I hate to think that, what do you call him, Dad, 'that little Austrian mustached, paperhanging bastard' will make us all look like we cannot run."

Freddie Wells leaned back in his chair, and then he stood up and walked round to where his son was sitting.

"Listen, Roland, what I am about to say may surprise you, but it's how I feel."

Roland took a deep breath. He was expecting the worst from his father.

He could not have been more wrong.

"You live to run, and run to live. I live to make this company what it is, and this company makes me. I am what I am. You're not me. In a way, I don't want you to be me. Ever since you won that first race at school and I realized that you were in a league of your own, your old headmaster and I realized that math and science were not where your head was, nor your heart. It was on the track, and in those spikes of yours. You run like the wind, Roland. You've made me very proud by joining the RAF Reserve, learning to fly, and scaring the hell out of your mother and me every time you disappear into the wild blue yonder."

"Dad, I am careful. I've been well trained by some of the best instructors in…"

"Hear me out, Son; I don't want to interrupt you, but just listen a little more. I realized when you left school that your mind and heart were elsewhere. That's okay. University was not on the cards, a profession in the law was not to be, but working with me was. When you joined the Godiva Harriers, I knew that I would be seeing less and less of you, and that the running track was your real home; plus, Jesse Birkett, once you met her…gosh, she's a great girl, and I need to chat about her, too. When you run, you run like the wind. I know that you are very upset on not being selected for the Olympics—you were a hair's breadth away. I'm really sorry, Son. You deserved a place. I'm no expert on anything to do with athletics, but I do know one thing—all my friends in the Freemasons who know athletics, tell me that you were robbed by people on the selection board who should have known better. So, to answer your question, go to Berlin with my blessing, give the team all the support you can, cheer your heart out, and I hope and pray that little Nazi's predictions for his master race to take all does not even come near to being true. I want you to do what you care about most."

Roland's eyes welled. His father had not spoken to him like this in several years. Every time he brought a cup and medal home, his dad was jubilant, full of praise, and clearly proud. But this was different; these words meant more to him than all the hoopla at home when he came home victorious, or even the runner up. This was different. He now saw his dad in a different light.

"Thanks, Dad." He paused, took a few breaths, and said, "It'll be just a few days. I'll scurry back as soon as the last British track event is over and…"

"Don't rush back, Roland, the business is not going to take off like your airplane. We'll all still be here. Enjoy yourself. I just have two requests. Please be careful in that plane. Carry some spare cans of oil, and for goodness sake, don't take chances with the weather. Weather can kill you. The other thing is this, and it is to do with the company."

Roland almost stood to attention in his seat. He then got up and looked his dad squarely in the eyes, something that both his parents has insisted on since he was a small boy—always make eye contact and never shift your eyes when addressing a person.

"Roland, I don't expect you to be the engineer, the designer, the super salesmen to Rolls Royce and our other customers, or manage the contracts and product deliveries. What I want from you is what you do really well—you inspire people. Great leadership is not about fact sheets and engineering drawings, it's about people and getting them to do things that they thought they were not capable of. You have great gifts of leadership, use them. What I want you to do is to continue what you do really well now—keep going down onto the shop floors and be with the men. They like you, listen to you, and you get the very most out of our people without a lot of pressure in ways that I never will in that old style factory management that I hate. Son, you inspire people. They also admire a great runner. They love to see your picture in the paper. Coventry Gear is going to need every ounce of your leadership skills and style. Just be yourself. This is all I ask. I'll take care of the business side. I can hire whoever we need to manage the expansion—accountants are ten a penny, lawyers grow on trees, and good draftsmen come running to us because we pay them well and, and this is my key point, Mr. Wells junior, the boss's son, is a man we can all trust and follow."

"Dad…"

"It's fine, Son, that's my message. Go to Berlin and give those Nazis hell, because before not too long, I predict that they will be dealing out their special version of hell to us and all our friends and allies…mark my word."

"Thank you. I won't let you down. As soon as I get back, I'll get to know every man on the shop floor more than I do now—I'll know the names of each of their wives, sweethearts, children, what they like and don't like, and most of all what we need to do to make life at Coventry Gear productive for them and for the company."

"You've got it, Son; you hit the nail right on the head. Now, when are you leaving?"

"Weather permitting, first thing in the morning. The forecast is good, if you can believe it."

"Which way will you head?"

"My usual route to the Oxford field via Banbury, then follow the main A40 to London, skirt round Blackbush field, and head across the South Downs to Dover. I'll leave the plane at a private grass strip I know near the town and take a taxi to the ferry. I'll head for Cologne, and then straight to Berlin."

"Give my best to the men you trained with. I've been following events in *The Times*. I love the man from America, Owens, Jesse Owens. He's just the best of the best; what an athlete! Hitler hates the man, just because he's black. If you get a chance, ask the little Nazi runt why he doesn't have blond hair and blue eyes, and what's with the mustache—ask him for me if he has acne!"

Roland laughed. His father was at his best vituperating over the Nazi leader.

"Dad, one quick question…what is with Jesse, and her languages? I thought that…"

"Glad you raised this. I was going to tell you. She's got a real talent for languages—no need to tell you that. I've heard her running rings 'round you when she flits from French to German, and then throws in a little Italian just to confuse you. She confuses me, I have to admit…at times I sometimes think that she's having a laugh at my expense and I don't understand a word!"

Roland laughed. "She does that all the time to me. I asked her the other day after we landed what she was saying while we were aloft in the Moth and you know what she said? 'You need to go read the English version of the poem that I was reciting in French while we were up in the sky, by the Canadian poet who was killed in the Great War, shortly after he wrote it—McGee's his name.' I have yet to read it."

"Well, Roland, what I'm about to tell you is very sensitive…for your ears only, no one else's. I don't ever even tell your mother about these things. She doesn't need to know, and wouldn't want her to know, in any case; she has enough things to worry about looking after your other siblings."

Roland sat down again. Freddie Wells retreated to his chair, sat down, and pulled out some papers from his desk drawer.

"The RAF people that were here are just part of this story. The Germans are building some very capable aircraft—bombers and fighters—some of them dive bombers. Nasty stuff. We know quite a lot about their basic designs, but we know little or nothing about their power plants—their engines. The Messerschmitt 109 and its derivatives are the really bad boys in this pack. Well, here's the story…we've acquired some of their engines, and they're over there at the field, hidden from view in the hangar on the far edge of the field—the one we own. The intelligence people down in London acquired them via various third parties, by what were clearly some pretty clever and devious means. Our job is to take them apart with some key people from Rolls Royce and find out just how good they are—what really makes them tick. And, furthermore, we need to find their weaknesses, who makes which components for them, and then the next stage—where they are made. We need to dissect these engines; they're in crates right now. We start work tomorrow. We have the manuals too—diagrams, maintenance schedules, and the like, but all in German. Jesse's role is to document each and every part in a very sensitive catalogue—classified is the word the security boys use who work with the intelligence collectors. She's going to get some special courses on German scientific and technical terms and German-English dictionaries from the good old Fatherland—again purloined, I gather, from various institutions. My job is to manage this with Rolls' key people. Her job is to make sure that we have everything documented in readable and understandable English. She's the ideal person. Your girlfriend, my employee and right-hand person, is going to do just that. Now, you must not tell a soul, do you understand, Son?"

For a few seconds Freddie Wells' hitherto friendly demeanor changed; he was transfixed, super serious, not quite threatening, but getting there.

"I understand, Dad. One question, can she and I discuss all this when we are…"

His father interrupted him.

"The answer is simple…only when you are in the hangar, doors closed and inside one of the rooms where each of the engines will be stripped down. All the windows have been sealed. I signed away my life with the intelligence people…you will be asked to do the same when you return from Berlin. Remember, discuss with no one except those cleared for this program. No loose chat with your pilot friends and no talk in an RAF mess because you think that they can be trusted. Remember that old saying, "loose lips, lose ships." I don't want any of us here at Coventry Gear falling foul of the security boys. If we do, we'll never be trusted again, and who knows what else might happen. Got the picture, Son? We've been given a great responsibility…let's live up to it."

"I've got it, Dad. Is that the paperwork in front of you?"

"Yes, we might as well do this now, no time like the present. Here, look this over, sign, date, and I'll witness. Two copies, one for us, and one for them. By the way, Jesse has signed, hope she hasn't breathed a word to you…has she?"

Roland gulped, not out of guilt, but because he now instantly realized that Jesse could keep a secret from him…she had known before him.

"Only that you and I needed to talk, and that the hangar was out of bounds. I think that she was giving me a subtle hint that I never picked up on. Otherwise, not a word, Dad; you have my word, I swear."

"I believe you, don't worry. She's the best. I need her here; otherwise, she could go to Berlin with you. Let's call it a day. I've got a meeting at the bank tomorrow—more loans to fund the expansion. I'll miss your departure at the field, but I'll see you at home in the morning. I've got a dinner tonight over at Armstrong Whitworth—we're going to discuss their needs. While you're away, I am going down to meet with A. V. Roe. Rolls and we are looking at the new bomber they are designing—very hush, hush, so far—a heavy long-range bomber. The code name is the Lancaster. Keep that tight, too. It will be able to fly into the heart of the Third Reich, or that's what they say. We want to use the new Merlin engine—four of them—hell of a power plant."

"I wish I had one on the front end of the Moth."

They both laughed.

"Let's quit." His father gathered up his papers, put them in his briefcase, straightened his tie in his office mirror, and buzzed his secretary on the intercom. The indispensable Miss Twigg came scuttling in, energy personified, the spirit and will of a twenty-five year old in the body of a fifty-five-year-old spinster.

"Is that all for the day, sir? Do you have everything you need for the evening meeting?"

"I'm fine, Rosemary." He never called her 'Rosy' like the rest of the staff. "Thanks for everything. You get on home. We'll work on the AVRO visit in the morning after I come back from the bank. I'm going to need my driver for that trip; I can do more work in the car rather than hang around waiting in railway stations."

"Goodnight, sir. Goodnight, Roland."

"Have a good evening," said Roland, noting that she would never dare call his father by his first name.

Father and son left the factory, climbed into their separate cars, with Frederick Wells driving his beloved Riley, and Roland in his Austin sports car.

Roland watched his father turn off toward Armstrong Whitworth's factory, and then headed for the Horse and Jockey and a pub dinner with Jesse. This would be their last night for a while...Berlin, next stop.

Chapter Seven
UNTER DEN LINDEN, BERLIN

As Roland rolled the Moth to obtain a better view of the center of Banbury from two thousand feet, with its famous Cross in the middle, and thoughts of Banbury cakes, he just could not recall the words of the poem by the Canadian McGee that Jesse had recited during their last flight. He made a mental note to learn them and recite them. The de Havilland 60 Moth with its Cirrus 1 engine purred along, scudding across the sky between cloud banks, with Roland following the landmarks below. His RAF training field on the outskirts of Oxford passed by, as he looked out for errant trainees, perhaps soloing for the first time, too excited to scan for other traffic. With 60 horsepower in front of him, Roland knew that he had quite a slow haul to Dover, but it beat driving and it certainly beat the tedium of trains. With a maximum level speed of about 91 miles per hour and enough range to cover 320 miles before refueling, he was feeling good as the Moth trundled across the sky.

He wished that he had the RAF trainer under his control as he overflew the outer western suburbs of London. The RAF Tiger Moth was a notch or two above his basic Moth. The DH 82A as it was officially designated flew at 109 miles per hour in level flight, and was a joy in which to execute aerobatics. The Tiger Moth's 130 horsepower engine gave Roland the extra power that he craved, but for now, the Moth was his (or his father's) and he was grateful that he could fly. But what of the new aircraft that his father mentioned…what was the Spitfire all about? What was the Merlin engine capable of? The Lancaster…a name he couldn't repeat and engines locked behind closed doors…and then his girlfriend, Jesse…what a woman. Suddenly he was back in a second to flying the Moth…no daydreaming. His RAF instructor's words came echoing into his mind like the words of the god—"Fly the airplane first, then navigate, and if you are lucky enough to have a radio, communicate, but above all else, fly the airplane!" The words were etched into his psyche. Aviate, navigate, and communicate!

The Downs were passed and the south coast appeared, and before he had gone thirty miles further, the White Cliffs of Dover stood out, and he turned along the coast toward the town, and then descended to find the grass strip tucked away near a golf course about five miles out of town to the north. He followed the main road north out of Dover at a thousand feet, rolled the airplane several times to look for the strip, and then spotted three brightly colored bi-planes in the field below and the outline of a landing strip. He figured out the wind, made a perfect entry downwind, eased the Moth gently into a turn to the base leg, and then onto a short final, put the nose down, and kept the Moth safely above stall speed as he eased all 1,200 pounds of his flimsy bird onto the grass. He kept the tail off the ground until he had near perfect directional control, eased off the power, and brought the stick back to let the tail wheel find the earth.

Life was good.

Next stop, the ferry, the train in Calais, France, and then onward into Germany. On the ferry and in the two trains that would take him across Europe to Berlin, Roland reflected on his farewell with Jesse at the field. It was passionate, full of warmth and mutual caring. He knew that they each were totally aware of one very simple fact—they were in love. For Jesse, the parting at Coventry was about Roland not taking risks and staying safe. His thoughts were about their future, how he adored her, and not about the risks of flying his light aircraft with no one but himself to save him if anything went wrong. Their mutual self-reliance was strengthened by the unspoken words that went beyond the kisses, the firm embraces, and telling eye exchanges; there was a fundamental bond of deep and abiding love and affection that transcended Jesse's worries about his well being and Roland's inner desires for her.

Unter den Linden is a street like Piccadilly and the Mall in London, Fifth Avenue in New York, and Constitution Avenue in Washington, DC. It's a household name, a meeting place of all meeting places with historical and maybe romantic connotations depending on the who, what, and when. The where, in this case, was already decided. Roland would meet his running friends at a beer garden just off the famous Berlin Street, owned by the redoubtable Lilly Stein, a formidable lady who on first appearance could have been anything that the imagination could conjure up—lady of the night, female *bon viveur*, alcoholic, the latest German fad of a Herr in Frau's attire, or whatever the imagination sought.

Roland could walk from his hotel, and the anticipation was overpowering. He had read the latest results in the *Frankfurter Zeitung* as he traveled east by train. Now the concierge at his hotel gave him the rest of the latest results—the locals were doing well, but not quite well enough. The shadow of the great Jesse Owens loomed over Berlin and the Reichstag, that monument to German unity and greatness. A black man from the middle of the American heartland had stolen the Games from the Aryan master race. How could this be? The Nazi propaganda machine had done its best to tone down and mollify the indelible facts, now inscribed in athletic history. The Olympian gods had come down from the Acropolis—Owens had been crowned. There could be no doubts—German honor, ambitions, and the Teutonic spirit had taken a severe beating, however, all was not over. Roland had come to watch the field events finale. He had interests and loyalties that supplanted any personal goals or ambitions that he had about competing in Berlin. For him, being there, right then, in the capital of the Third Reich was to support those whose friendship he cared for most.

Cheers went up when he appeared in the elegant garden bar at the rear of the beer hall. Roland beamed. The four of them stood like a solid phalanx of British athletic manhood—cheerful, ebullient, and totally unabashed by their surroundings—Godfrey Rampling, Freddie Wolff, Bill Roberts, and Godfrey Brown made an impressive sight. Casual in dress, relaxed in manner, and totally unassuming, they were nonetheless a sight that no observer could characterize other than splendid. They all beamed when they caught sight of Roland. Hands were shook, greetings exchanged, and a huge beer mug thrust into Roland's hand by Godfrey Rampling. Roland knew that with the big event yet to come, they would be restraining their intake, but for now, it was simple—a good German beer was going down five thirsty throats.

"What time is the race, I haven't seen a program yet?" asked Roland.

"Two o'clock tomorrow afternoon, and guess what?" said Godfrey Rampling. "You won't believe it, but Don Finlay's 110-meter hurdles final is after our final by one hour. It'll give us enough time to shower, celebrate, and get in place to watch him!" They all laughed.

"Ever the optimist," said Freddie Wolff. "We just have to remember to hand over the baton in our excitement." They all laughed.

"We haven't forgotten yet, and we're not going to start now," said Rampling, clearly the leader of this quartet on overdrive for tomorrow's final of the 4-by-400-meter relay.

"Well," said Roland, " there's going to be one English voice in the crowd that plans to outdo all those German voices when the gun goes off at three; it's called the man from Coventry and, by golly, you men are going to have the race of your lives. I can feel it in the air. You're all ready—you look terrific!"

There was a spontaneous outburst of "thanks" from the four hopefuls that were now the pride of the British athletics team. A lot now rested on them, and Don Finlay.

All heads turned because it suddenly became apparent that the whole beer hall was muted, almost stunned.

Rampling said just one word, "Jesse."

In the entrance to the outer garden stood James Cleveland Owens, better known as Jesse Owens, the new four times Olympic gold medalist. The only word to describe him was 'magnificent.' He stood tall and handsome in a two-piece beige suit and cream open neck shirt. He lifted his hand and waved greetings to the British four and their new companion. Without any cue from Rampling, the five of them burst into a round of loud applause. The Germans in the hall were stultified—here was the man, a black born in the American South whose middle name was the same as the city his family left for to escape the pressures of the South and find a new life and better opportunities in Cleveland,

Ohio; the man who had in four monumental races over the previous days systematically took apart the Third Reich's belief in its own athletic invincibility. Without regard to the swastika laden hall, and the brown shirted onlookers positioned at various stations around the hall, the whole gathering followed the British lead—they stood as one and simply clapped, and clapped, and clapped.

Jesse strode up to the five men and clasped their hands one after another, with a big broad smile.

"Meet a great friend and supporter of ours from Britain, Roland Wells, a Godiva Harrier from the great city of Coventry; I guess what Americans would call our heartland, slap in the middle of England."

"Good to meet a fellow athlete, Roland, and better still to meet a friend of these four—they're the best—no that's not quite right—they're the best of the best."

Roland smiled, and said, "It's an honor, a great honor to meet you Mr. Owens...Jesse, if I may call you that, please."

"You certainly can. It's my pleasure."

"My dad and I have been following your every race. Congratulations! You were fantastic...we were waiting for the radio to come on with each of your races. The BBC did a wonderful job of commentating. The 100 meters was electrifying. The BBC man was in shock—he was so exhilarated. My dad got out from his desk in the office and jumped for joy. I am not kidding."

"I want to meet your dad, please."

"He would love to be here, but he has to run our family business."

"That's a shame, what do you all do, may I ask, please?" asked Owens; but no sooner had Roland begun to answer, when Bill Roberts and Godfrey Brown put their arms up, and Bill said, "Well, look who's come to join the party."

Eyes turned.

Marching toward them with the stride of a military man was the pride of the Royal Air Force's athletics team, and the finest 110-meter hurdler Britain had ever produced—Donald "Don" Osborne Finlay—a man with a mission, to better the bronze medal that he won in the 1932 Los Angeles Olympic Games, commissioned as a pilot in the RAF a year before the Berlin Games, after joining as a boy apprentice in 1925.

"Jesse, what a great pleasure, and Roland, you made it...great to see you, thanks so much for coming...we're honored; so glad you could break away. You've met Roland, Jesse?"

"Sure have. He's from Coventry and I'm from Cleveland, and not the Cleveland you all know—I'm from the place in Ohio named after your Cleveland."

They all laughed.

"Well, Don, I want to tell you that whatever goes on with the American competition in the 110-meter hurdles, my heart is going to be with you tomorrow."

"Thanks, Jesse, you're very kind. I really do want to better my LA performance in '32, and, oh, I shouldn't say this, but all the folks back at my base in England want me to add a little extra beyond what I did in the Empire Games in '34."

Finlay was referring modestly to his gold medal in the 120-yard hurdles in the British Empire Games in 1934, two years each side of the last and current Olympic Games.

"We're all with you, Don, never fear, and whatever the outcome, we know one thing—you'll give it your all."

"Don and I have been chatting a lot while we were out there training and off the field. I want to tell you guys how much I appreciate your friendship and support. This has not been an easy ride for me. My old track coach back at Fairmount Junior High, my best and dearest friend ever, Charles Riley, said my biggest problem would never be running, but being accepted. You five…sorry, Roland…you six have given me a lot of hope and faith in people. I just want to say thank you. You're the best."

"You don't have to say that, Jesse. We all think the world of you." As Finlay was about to add a few more words, Jesse became a little emotional and lowered his head, as if overcome.

He then looked them all in the eye, one by one. "You know, guys, when I went to Ohio State, I won a lot, but you know, I had to live off campus, eat at 'black only' restaurants when the college team traveled, and it was often worse than that. You guys have accepted me as one of your own and I tell you, I love you for it, you're my brothers."

The six Britons were overcome.

Roland broke the ice, the newcomer, the one who had not spent the past several weeks watching how the rest of the whites in the American team related to Jesse—to say off hand was a huge understatement.

"Your four gold medals will stand for all time, long after all these things have come to pass, believe you me, Jesse, one day, well…one day, those people are going to recognize you not just for the true hero that you are and the greatest athlete, but a man that we should all try to follow. It's a great honor to meet and know you. I wish my dad was here—he'd love to shake you by the hand."

"Thanks, Roland, that's mighty nice of you."

"Jesse, if you ever come to England, you have to meet Roland's dad. He's quite a character. We all love him. He hates the Nazis with a vengeance. He sent me a telegram, Roland, arrived just a few hours ago, wishing me all the best for the final."

"I'd love to bring my wife and daughter to England."

"You're married?" said Roland.

"Sure am, high school sweetheart, my beloved Minnie. She's the best. We married last year, but we did have our daughter Gloria in 1932. We got ahead of ourselves, so to speak, but with help from our folks it all worked out in the end. She's my biggest and best supporter. You'll all love her."

Don Finlay changed the subject because he could sense that Jesse felt a little overcome, overwhelmed by genuine friendship, warmth from whites that he had clearly never ever experienced before.

"What about food, gents? I don't think any of us can stand the thought of eating back at the Olympic Center. How about we treat ourselves to a good meal before tomorrow's races—lots of protein and calories? We're going to need them."

"Great idea, Don," Rampling added. "Any ideas, gents?"

Roland said that there was a great place near to his hotel, a short walk from the beer garden, recommended by the concierge at his hotel.

"Let's do it," said Jesse.

The seven men left the beer hall. It was a symbolic departure. It was not lost on the Germans. They all knew who Owens was. His photos had been all over every major German newspaper. Even the racist Aryans present who eschewed Hitler's propaganda could not help but notice that the six English athletes looked like they were totally at home in the company of the great black American athlete. They were right. They were.

The cool evening air on the Unter den Linden was invigorating. There was a pleasant breeze wafting down Germany's most famous street. The Reichstag was all lit up, the floodlights illuminating the façade, and the Brandenburg Gate's dramatic architecture added a Wagnerian atmosphere to a city that was high on athletic frenzy.

What would tomorrow bring?

As the seven athletes sat down for their dinner, only one thought was in the minds of the British relay team and Britain's finest hurdler. Could they succeed? Could they emulate Jesse Owens? Could they redeem other losses, and bring home a little glory, glory that it would take many years, indeed decades, before Jesse Owens would be truly honored by his country, a new generation that did not have prejudice in its heart.

Tonight the moment was with these seven good men. Tonight friendships would be made that would last forever. No one could ever take this away from them, not prejudice, not bigotry, not evil propaganda, and not the simple passage of time and the distance that would eventually separate them on the conclusion of the Games.

Chapter Eight
A DAY TO REMEMBER
A CROWNING GLORY

The British relay team faced both strong American and German teams. At breakfast the relay team and Finlay learned that Hitler would be attending this day. The 4-by-400-meter relay final was a star attraction. For Godfrey Rampling, it was his swan song. At six feet one inch and about twelve stones (76 kg), he was an ideal size. He had won a relay silver medal in 1932. This was his last chance for the ultimate accolade—gold. He was the strength of the team, but a chain is only as strong as its weakest link and Rampling had three superb athletes to complement his undoubted key role in the team. At breakfast that morning, the expectation could be cut with a knife. Rampling's military training shone through. He kept his team focused, steady, but relaxed enough so as not to exhaust themselves with unnecessary expenditure of nervous energy.

Don Finlay had joined them for breakfast, hoping that the quiet confidence that they exuded would rub off on him. It did. They distracted themselves with chatter over the newspapers and reviewing the previous days' races and results. Rampling and Finlay were occupied by comparing personal notes on their military careers to date and training. At 27, Rampling was at one level the more experienced man, having been trained at the Royal Military Academy and then became a Royal Artillery officer. He had good coaches, particularly the renowned Walter George, who trained him at the Royal Military Academy Sandhurst. Don Finlay had become an RAF officer via a technical apprenticeship as an enlisted airman and had been commissioned later, his intelligence, leadership potential, and ability to become a pilot spotted early on in his time in the RAF. Today service rivalries were irrelevant. Both men were joined in one pursuit—victory. Don's strength lay in his innate courage and fortitude. As a hurdler, he had tremendous will power.

Roland knew what it was like as the tension built from first thing in the day until the moment when all would be decided—the starter's gun and the dash to the finishing line. Today he had no spikes, no running vest, and no limbering up exercises to accomplish in the morning as a preamble to the one short training session before the afternoon races. He stayed away from the team—they didn't need a distraction or more encouragement. He had a great seat near the front on the final stretch just before the finish line, and he planned to let them know he was there—his voice was distinctive and carried. He would cheer his heart out for both events.

Roland was close to Don Finlay—they had been friends for some time—often rivals in numerous track events and club competitions. Like Rampling, Don Finlay was born in May, 1909—they were the same age. Roland was very much the junior member in age, six years younger than the oldest member of the team. He had yet to reach his athletic peak, one of the chief reasons why he had not made the British Olympic Team—another four years and he would be at the height of his athletic prowess. Flying had also brought them closer—as a weekend warrior in the RAF Reserves, Roland had done his basic flying training with Don. Although older, Don had spent several years in the ranks before being selected for a commission and pilot training. Roland had enormous respect for Don's accomplishments as a runner and as a pilot, and also someone who had not received all the benefits Roland enjoyed with a wealthy, successful father and a private education. Roland respected what Don had achieved to break the mold of a slower start in life and then achieve this level of athletic achievement and a commission in the Royal Air Force. All were great accomplishments for a man who started life as a boy apprentice.

As the day wore on and the noon hour passed, a light lunch was taken by the five athletes. Their short training session had been very good, including a final baton passing practice. Roland was seated in his fine seat with a commanding view of the finish line when a tap on the shoulder from behind made him turn—there was Jesse Owens.

"Can I come over and join you?"

"Of course, step over. You're okay…there's a seat right here."

"Who are you putting your money on?" Jesse joked.

"It's going to be tough, Jesse. Your team is good. It's going right down to the wire."

"Roland, you're right on the money. I don't want to call it."

They chatted in between the half dozen events that preceded the 3 o'clock 4-by-400-meter relay race.

Rampling, Wolff, Roberts, and Brown appeared from the underground walkway that led from the changing areas. Security was intense. Everywhere there seemed to be swastika-wearing guards. The Reich's chancellor was in position in his box above and behind Roland and Jesse. He looked ominous in his dark and very dull suit. He hardly smiled, taciturn, and talked with his Propaganda Minister Goebbels, a most ominous man with a skeletal appearance and sallow, hollow cheeks.

The Nazis were expecting a victory in the relay final. Their news reports had overdone the buildup of their team—it was over the top. They now had everything to lose, or at least that's what Jesse and Roland were hoping.

The foursome limbered up, striding and stretching, and generally loosening up their muscles. The main opposition, the German and American teams, were performing similar movements, with the Germans making exaggerated gyrations as if they were trying to tell the spectators, look we're not only different, we're the best.

The Games' marshals ushered the competitors to their pre-race stations. The starter was checking his pistol and inserting the rounds.

The British had a plan. Rampling, the strongest runner by far was to run the second leg, and then hand over to Bill Roberts. The idea was that Rampling would make up any deficit and, hopefully, give the final two sufficient leeway to keep ahead.

The clock moved toward 3 P.M. The teams took their start positions, and got ready for the gun. The crowd hushed. Roland glanced round at the official box—Hitler looked nervous. His henchmen surrounding him were silent and had stone faces.

The gun went off, and so did the runners on the first of four, four hundred-meter legs. As they rounded the bend for the first hand-off Roland stood up and cheered loudly. As he handed over to Rampling, the records would show that Great Britain was a full eight meters behind the two leaders, the United States and Germany.

Roland shouted, "Go, Godfrey, go."

Godfrey Rampling ran like the wind. He excelled all expectations. With eight meters to make up and place the British team back in contention, he had to run the race of his life. He did. The crowd was mesmerized as he rounded the bend, each stride catching the American, and then, he overtook the leader with a spurt of energy that defied any predictions. He came to the hand-off, it was perfectly executed, and the commentators were telling the world that Britain had gone from eight meters down when Rampling took over to a three-meter lead when the baton left his hand. It had been a stupendous effort. The British held their lead; the crowd stood up and roared. The Americans tried valiantly to make up the difference, but at the tape the British passed it first, and officially two seconds ahead of the Americans in second place.

They had won gold. The silver went to the United States.

Roland Wells and Jesse Owens stood and cheered and cheered. It was a race of a lifetime. The official time was 3 minutes, 9 seconds, a new European record. Rampling's time for his crucial lap was 46.6 seconds.

The two spectators were overwhelmed with joy. On the field, the foursome huddled in a group in a tight knot of self congratulation.

Back in Coventry, Frederick Wells took his smartly folded handkerchief from his top pocket to wipe away a tear. He was so overjoyed. The BBC radio commentator had reduced his audience to an emotional state close to collapse by the time the finishing tape was broken. It was one of the greatest Olympic races of all time, one for the history books. Rampling was to say later, "I never felt as good as that day. I just seemed to float 'round the track, passing people without effort."

The 'Austrian paperhanger,' as Frederick Wells dubbed Hitler, was not amused. At the medal presentation he was visibly miffed, ungracious in defeat. When the British national anthem was played and *God Save the King* echoed around the stadium, he could hardly hold himself still, as he was clearly shaking with anger. Such was the nature of the leader of the Third Reich.

The medal ceremony was dominated by the playing of the British national anthem. As *God Save the King* echoed around the Berlin Stadium, the four British athletes were decorated with their gold medals. Hitler was nowhere to be seen. The 'Master Race' was in third place. The Americans were gracious in receiving their silver medals, congratulating the British on a great race. The Anglo-American camaraderie was self-evident, sporting goodwill at its best. The Germans looked angry, with unconcealed disappointment hiding an arrogance that was unmistakable.

Jesse used his special pass to escort Roland back to the locker rooms.

The meeting was eventful.

There was much hand shaking, back slapping, and good cheer. The American silver medalists joined the British team for a hearty round of mutual congratulations. This was interrupted by the British team manager, who wanted them to go outside again for a series of press photographs. This they did.

When all had collected themselves after the adrenalin burst of first the race itself and then the excitement of winning, Roland very gently mentioned that Don's turn was close at hand. Did they all feel up to coming out once they had changed?

The answer was never in doubt. The four gold medalists quickly showered and changed into their British Olympic blazers and flannel trousers, and headed for the stands where Roland and Jesse had reserved four additional seats.

Don Finlay was on the field limbering up. The 110-meter hurdles race would be over in a flash. His race was about sheer unadulterated energy, unleashed in a matter of a few seconds. The rhythm and stride over the hurdles was all important. His event combined the power of the 100-meter sprint with the taxing addition of striding over those hurdles.

All eyes in the row of six were fixed on Donald Finlay. The gun exploded, and Don's energy exploded with it.

He ran the race of his life, just pipped at the finishing post to win the silver medal. His six supporters stood and cheered and, once the noise subsided, left their seats to make their way back to the locker rooms to meet Don and congratulate him.

Back in England, two very fine RAF senior officers cheered in office of the more senior. Air Chief Marshal Sir Hugh Dowding, air officer commander in chief, fighter command, turned to the air officer commanding 11 Group Fighter Command, the New Zealander Air Vice Marshal Keith Park and said, "Well, he's done it…a silver medal for Britain and great credit to the service. Send him my congratulations please, Keith."

"I certainly will, sir."

The two discussed other business and Park said to Dowding that he was going up to Coventry in the morning to get the results of the analysis of the German engines.

Park departed the HQ at Bently Priory near Stanmore, and headed back to his own headquarters at Uxbridge. It had been a long day already that started early and would finish late.

In Berlin the celebrations were just starting. It would be a night to remember.

Leni Riefenstahl made a movie of the 1936 Berlin Olympic Games. Despite its original propagandist intent, the film was generally recognized as a masterpiece for its time. The highlight of the film, by worldwide popular acclaim, is the part dealing with the 4-by-400-meter relay final. Rampling's herculean second leg stole the show—it shows him coming back from behind to give his team what was to be the winning lead.

By the early hours of the following day, the British athletes and their American friend were exhausted. They all slept until midday.

As they prepared to depart Berlin, Roland offered Don Finlay a ride in the Moth from Dover back to his base. He gratefully accepted.

The only sad part of the final day was the parting of the ways with Jesse Owens. They all made it clear to the American that this was not the end, but the beginning. For Don Finlay, Roland Wells, and Jesse Owens this was the beginning of a lifetime friendship that time and distance would not breach.

Little did any of them realize there in Berlin, in the summer of 1936, what lay ahead in just three short years. The world would change in ways, the likes of which none of these young men would ever have predicted.

Back in Coventry, two much older men knew what the end game was.

Chapter Nine
SEPTEMBER 3, 1939
COVENTRY GEAR, COVENTRY, ENGLAND

The Coventry Gear management team was huddled around the radio in Frederick Wells' office. It was a somber gathering.

"Can you tune the radio, Rosemary, please? There's a little too much static. If we're going to hear bad news, we might as well make sure that we hear every word, and when you have a minute, I would really love another cup of tea please, though I think I may need something stronger after what Neville Chamberlain's going to tell us all."

There was a muffled sound of agreement from the assembled team. The radio came alive.

"This is the BBC, and this is Alvar Liddell. Here is a special broadcast by the Prime Minister, the Right Honorable Neville Chamberlain, speaking from 10 Downing Street in London." There was a pause.

Neville Chamberlain's chilling voice came over the airwaves.

"I am speaking to you from the Cabinet Room of 10 Downing Street. This morning, the British Ambassador in Berlin handed the German government a final note, stating that unless we heard from them by 11 o'clock that they were prepared at once to withdraw their troops from Poland, a state of war would exist between us. I have to tell you now, that no such undertaking has been received, and that, consequently, this country is at war with Germany."

"Well, that's that," said Frederick Wells. "If he had listened to Winston three years ago, we would not now be in this dire situation. We'd be better prepared. Well, it's no use crying over spilt milk. We've faced the likes of Adolf Hitler before. All right, gentlemen, let's get to it. We've got a lot of work to do in preparation for tomorrow's meeting in London at the Ministry of Aircraft Production. The people from Rolls will be there, together with AVRO, Hawker, and Vickers, and I gather several of the other lead subcontractors for the Spitfire, Hurricane, and Lancaster production issues. I'll need all the data we've got so that I can advise on what our best effort increased production rate can be. We'll have to match whatever AVRO, Hawker, and Supermarine are told to produce."

"Any idea, sir, what the numbers might be?" said George.

"I'm guessing a minimum of at least five times current production levels, maybe even higher. We're in trouble. The Luftwaffe are producing the ME 109 and their bomber fleet like there's no tomorrow."

"We're going to have to produce a detailed manpower plan. The lower end people are easy to find, but, sir, the skilled draftsmen and precision gear cutters, that's a tough issue—they do not grow on trees. We've talked about finding several hundred highly skilled people in a matter of weeks. That's unprecedented."

"I know, you're quire correct, but somehow, gentlemen, we going to have to do it, otherwise this country is in deep trouble. We're exposed. If we can't defend these islands, the rest of the world will go down with us."

"Do you want to address the work force at 1 o'clock as planned?" said the senior shop floor manager.

"Yes, please, I need to let everyone know what the score is, and where we are headed. Above all, I need to tell them my worst fears as well—we need to increase security and get ready with better firefighting equipment and the like. This war will be different from anything that we've ever known before."

"Yes, sir, we'll make an announcement over the Tannoy. Do you want everyone?"

"Everyone, please, except the gate guards and the special security detail out at the field for the hangar—I'll speak with these people in smaller groups over the next day or so. I've asked Roland to be the lead for all personnel matters. We are going to have to heighten security awareness and check who's coming in and out of the factory 'round the clock, similarly with vehicle movements. I'm expecting some additional security rules for us from London."

The team departed, with the exception of Roland.

"Do you have a minute, Dad?"

"Can you be brief, Son?"

"Dad, I need to talk about my flying and the RAF. They need me now."

"I'd prefer not to discuss this right now if you don't mind, please, Roland. I've got a lot to do before the 1 o'clock meeting with our people. Just bear in mind, Son, that you're crucial, not just because you're my son and would take over if anything happened to me, but also you're the person our work force looks up to—I know you and everyone here were disappointed about the Olympic Games place that did not come your way, but they all understand that—you're their local hero. Let's talk later if you don't mind and, by the way, will you call your mother and tell her not to wait for me for dinner."

"Yes, Dad," said Roland, somewhat downhearted and hiding his inner disappointment that his father would not give him time to discuss his dilemma.

Roland felt that he owed it to the country, to his family, and to himself to immediately seek to be recalled for full-time active service with a regular RAF fighter squadron. He was already feeling the tinge of not fulfilling what he considered his duty—what would his fellow reserve pilots think of him if he did not volunteer immediately, and wait for a telegram from the Air Ministry summoning him to full-time active duty? The specter of cowardice went through his mind. He was ready for action, whatever it entailed, wherever, and whenever.

Frederick Wells was always impressive when addressing his loyal work force. He was one of the most respected industrialists in Coventry and the Midlands. He was known for his charity work and he took good care of all his people. He was always fair, and led by example. He worked harder than anyone and they all knew it. He drove a fine Riley car and had a very comfortable house on the outskirts of Coventry, but he was not ostentatious in any way, nor was he vain or conceited about his success since he first set up the business. Many others had shared his success thanks to his generosity and desire to see others succeed.

Chamberlain's announcement had been heard on the Tannoy system throughout the factory. After explaining what he thought the consequences of war with Germany would mean for Coventry Gear, and the impact on each individual and their families, he paused for a moment and gathered himself.

"Well, men, I now want to apprise you all of what my personal best assessment is of what might happen to us all here in Coventry. The Nazis have made it very clear that bombing civilian targets is part of their strategy—they devastated poor Poland and had no regard for the lives of innocent civilians—women and children were not spared in their monstrous blitzkrieg. They are ruthless. The Hun will not spare us here in our island bastion. I predict that they will bomb the industrial centers, such as the Midlands. Unlike no war before, we will all be on the frontline with the possibility of blitzkrieg attack from the air. The team here at Coventry Gear will start preparing for the very worst contingencies—we are going to need better firefighting and damage control equipment and train many of you to take charge if we are attacked—I talked to the Lord Mayor at dinner recently about this possibility. The fire brigade in Coventry may have its hands full in ways that none of us could ever have anticipated. Looking at the newsreels coming out of Poland, it's very clear to me what we can expect. Bottom line, men, we'll be implementing a whole range of wartime measures—security, firefighting, and the like. The work force is going to multiply many times over and very quickly. I want you all to help the newcomers—make them feel at home and help them all you can, please. Many of you will be involved in training, and even you younger ones fresh out of school are very soon going to find yourselves in leadership positions on the shop floors. Now, let me explain what I anticipate will be the new working routine. It's yet to be decided by the management team, but I think we'll be operating 'round the clock, most likely three 8-hour shifts. It's the only way that we can increase production. One long day shift will not hack it, even if we work from seven in the morning until eight at night. Exhausting everyone is counterproductive. But it will mean that one in three shifts will be a night shift for you all. When you're off work, please, whatever you do, get plenty of rest. I don't want to find that our accident rate goes up. That would not be good for anyone. I know many of you like a drink; I certainly do, but please cut down on pub time. You'll need all the energy you can muster. Now are there any questions? I've got about fifteen minutes. Who's first?"

Frederick Wells answered a battery of questions from his men. A lot were clearly already thinking about their families and what would happen to their wives and children if Coventry was attacked. Wells gave them straight answers to straight questions and did not dodge any issues. If longer hours were necessary, then people would be compensated, naturally, he said. He talked about local volunteer work to supplement the fire service and special constabulary.

When questions were over, Frederick Wells made one final comment.

"It's not going to be easy. This will be no picnic, mark my words, but if we all pull together we will endure, believe you me. We're a tough bunch and none of us are going to let that little jackbooted Nazi walk over any of us. We will produce what the government wants and what our airmen will need to fight the Luftwaffe. Thank you all, and God save the King."

There was a unanimous and spontaneous response, "God save the King."

The men dispersed and Frederick Wells headed back to his office and the first of many meetings in preparation for the trip to London in the morning.

Roland gathered his shop floor managers, for each of the main gear cutting workshops and then called a joint meeting with all the foremen and charge hands. He went over what was likely in terms of the expansion impacts—particularly training and supervision. There would be additional promotions from the shop floors to supervisory positions, and he would implement in the next few days a plan to organize better security and firefighting training. All that he said resonated well, and he then took his managers aside for a separate meeting to discuss physical expansion—building new workshops and the new machine tools required to increase production. His father and his other top managers would want answers to all these questions.

Roland had a late pub dinner with Jesse Birkett. Like him, she was recovering from the impact of the Declaration of War. She had a busy day putting together more documentation for the London meeting on the latest engineering and technical assessments of what may prove, she said, to be the last pieces of German equipment that the intelligence people will acquire. Roland made an observation with which she was in total agreement, "It's unlikely that we'll get anything out of Poland. Most of the Luftwaffe stayed intact, so there's virtually no wreckage, and even if there was, we'd never get it now that the Nazis occupy Poland."

He wanted to discuss his personal problem with Jesse. She was very sympathetic, but also quite direct. "Roland, if I were you, I wouldn't raise this again with your father. He's totally preoccupied—he's got more on his plate than anyone. I wouldn't worry him right now. He needs you badly."

"You're right, Jesse," he said downhearted. "Maybe he'll listen after a good night's sleep and we can talk about it in the morning in the car going down to London?"

"Roland, my love, you're not listening. I don't think you should raise this matter again with him until the war situation becomes clearer."

Roland dropped her off at her parent's home in Keresley, gave her a big goodnight kiss, and headed home. His father was in his study working, the door was closed, and his mother had already retired to bed.

Maybe, in the morning, Roland said to himself.

The drive to London was uneventful, with Rosemary sitting in the front with the company driver and taking copious shorthand dictation that Frederick Wells was firing at her like a machine gun, with letters and memoranda to a large number of subcontractors and prime contractors, internal company memoranda, and a letter to the local Member of Parliament, inviting him to visit the factory and have dinner with Wells and his managers. Roland started to discuss his issue at one point. He was cut off by Rosemary in the most tactful manner possible under the circumstances, turning with note pad in hand and asking him, "Roland, may I take dictation for you, too, sir. I know you've got a lot of new memoranda to get out for the shop floor managers and the plans for the new buildings." She raised her eyebrows at the same time, and rolled her eyes just enough to give Wells junior a clear message—I think that this is not a good time to irritate your father.

The Whitehall meetings went well. On the way back to Coventry in the early evening, Frederick made some terse comments about German capabilities. According to the Air Ministry assessment, the Messerschmitt 109E and 110 were highly capable, and although the Germans had made some requirement and acquisition errors with the bombers—the Junkers 87 and 88, Dornier 17, and Heinkel—the fact remained that numbers count hugely. Could Britain cope with the potential onslaught in the worst case that the numbers indicated?

Roland seized this opportunity to jump in from a different angle and use his father's comments as a reason for supporting his personal wishes.

"Dad, what will count is not just our production rates to match theirs, and hopefully with far superior airplanes, but also much better trained pilots. The RAF needs me, Dad. I know I'm a Reservist, but I have as many, if not more, flying hours than most of the more experienced regulars. I am fully qualified on the Spitfire and am eligible to become an instructor pilot."

His father bristled. He took off his horn-rimmed glasses and stared his son directly in the eyes. In the front, the chauffeur and Miss Twigg exchanged knowing glances, as if fireworks were about to explode in the back of the car.

"Roland, I have no problem with you doing reservist flight training, instructing others at weekends and so forth, but—and this is a big but—your place is at Coventry Gear. Why? It's very simple. You and all the employees at Coventry Gear, with the exception of totally unskilled workers, have been designated critical war production personnel, and are exempt from any form of military service. Roland, you are not going into the RAF as a full-time active pilot, and that's the end of that. The government has decided for you."

"Or have you decided for the government, is that what you really mean?"

There was deathly silence. The tension in the car was intense.

Roland had not remembered Jesse's advice.

Frederick was not about to dress down his own son in front of his secretary and driver. He took a few deep breaths, but he made one thing clear.

"Roland, that's the end of the matter. Please drop the subject." He then played a card, which his son could not counter. "I'm tired; we've all had a very long day. Please leave it alone, if you don't mind."

"Yes, Dad, I'm sorry."

Rosemary breathed a quiet sigh of relief. After the two Wells men were dropped off at the house, the chauffeur looked at Rosemary as soon as they left the driveway of the Tamworth Road house and said, "Well, the old man certainly kept the lid on that one. I thought he was going to give Roland both barrels."

"Not in his nature, Charles."

"I'm glad."

"Mind that cat. Don't run over that black cat for goodness sake, terrible bad luck."

"I missed it. I hope Roland keeps quiet."

"He will…," then she paused, "for the time being."

Chapter Ten
THEIR FINEST HOUR
THE BATTLE OF BRITAIN

"Never in the course of human conflict has so much been owed by so many to so few"

—*Winston Churchill*

"Keep in formation, for goodness sake. Watch your attitude indicator and keep the ball centered. Maintain 12,000 feet, and heading 180—repeat one eight zero on the heading. If you stray, Gerry will have you for lunch. I don't want to see any random firing. Only fire when you are so close that you can see the whites of their eyes. I don't want anyone running out of ammo because of random bursts. Do you all read me?"

Finlay's flight of Spitfires from number 54 Squadron based at Hornchurch all replied in the affirmative over the radio to their esteemed leader.

It was July 11, 1940, a cloudy day, when the Luftwaffe lost twenty aircraft to the RAF's 6. Finlay's flight landed without loss. They had not scored any victories.

They had been over the English Channel protecting shipping in the Portsmouth and Portland areas. He had forbidden any of his crews from chasing enemy aircraft back toward France for fear of running out of fuel and then being forced to ditch in the Channel.

"It's bad enough if you lose a valuable aircraft; that will not please me, the squadron commander, or the wing commander, but if you end up dead in the Channel, we've all lost a valuable pilot—do you all understand?" said Finlay in the hut where the post operations debriefings took place, with the intelligence officers interrogating the aircrew on what transpired and what they learned about the enemy.

"Once the Intel boys and girls have finished with you, back to the ready room; we're still on standby for another sortie, and we need to talk. I want you all to stay alive. I hate writing obituaries."

Once they were settled, mugs of tea in hand, Finlay reminded them of the key flight characteristics of the ME 109 and ME 110, and why they needed to exploit the key maneuvering characteristics of the Spitfire, since in straight and level flight there was little to choose between the top speeds of the opposing aircraft. He stressed a series of tactics that would give them an advantage. He emphasized, "You have to get in close before firing—so close that you can see your rounds penetrating their machines. Standing back will not work. All that stuff you learned in flight training is wrong. The ranges are far too optimistic. Your two 20-millimeter cannons and four 303s will more than do the job—just get in close with the bombers—get right up to them, and then let them have it, the rear gunners will often just not see you until the last minute. Now, when we're going after the bombers, I will let you know who I want to hang back and look for their fighters. If they're high, I don't want us getting jumped by their escorts. Depending on the sun, we'll try to get them in front of us with the sun behind us whenever we can, and the aircraft I keep back will be high enough to see the enemy fighter escorts. Remember, stay tight, don't get seduced into going off on your own and then get jumped by a bunch of enemy aircraft that you never saw—sure way to get yourself killed. Once we do get in a mêlée with their fighters, I want to make sure that we know where all their aircraft are before we engage—no surprises. Got it?"

They all nodded. One of the more experienced pilots added that he thought that some of the RT procedures were not clear, "Only report a contact if you are sure—panic calls waste fuel and valuable time; check that your windshield is always clean before getting airborne—a dead bug can look like the dot of a distant ME 109."

They all laughed.

"It's no laughing matter, men, if that bug is really the enemy—you have all got to get your aircraft recognition up to snuff," Finlay stressed. "You've all got the recognition cards—test each other until you know everything that there is to know about each aircraft. I'm having a quiz before every sortie starting tomorrow. Anyone who scores badly buys the beer!"

Finlay then laid out what he thought might happen over the next several days based on the intelligence reassessment from Eleven Group Headquarters at Uxbridge. He said that all the stations in the 'Group' would be on a high state of alert—their own station at Hornchurch would be at maximum readiness with Tangmere, Kenly, Biggin Hill, Northholt, North Weald, and Debden. They were at the pointy end of the spear.

Finlay's flight sergeant interrupted and informed the flight leader that they had been 'stood down' for the rest of the day—they would be on call at twilight the next morning—the Luftwaffe were expected to go after more convoys in the Channel and attack the Naval ports on the south coast.

"Very good, Staff Sergeant. We're going to use the rest of the daylight to go up and practice what I just preached. I'm going to emphasizes three things—formation flying close together, breaking into four echelons to different altitudes, and then regrouping for a mass attack once we figure out where and what is the fighter escort. Shooting down bombers is the goal, men. It's the bombers that will destroy our ports, ships, and kill people on the ground. We kill their fighters when they may kill us—we go after the bombers first and the fighter escorts when we have no choice."

The men collected their life vests, parachutes, and personal gear.

"Oh, and one more thing, men…when we get to altitude, I'll call the altitudes on the outbound leg. I want each group within the flight to scan for targets. Get used to doing this as a routine—never ever stop scanning, remember to use your peripheral vision, don't stare at the horizon at one place, or stare up or down, scan slowly across the sky through the whole clock, and call targets as you've been trained—one to twelve o'clock, high, level, or low. Get it."

"Yes, sir," they said collectively.

Once airborne, Finlay was in his element. He put the whole flight through a series of drills, each group within the flight changing roles and altitudes. He made sure that he had one experienced pilot in each of the flight groups. Finlay called the overall shots, but he had his leaders trained to take full responsibility for their roles and sectors. He was very conscious of one critical fact—if he was shot down or disabled during a mêlée, he wanted his leaders to take over. He'd appointed a veteran flight lieutenant as his deputy flight commander in the event of the worst case happening to him. Finlay was a realist.

Several days later on July 25 and 28, this training paid off.

Fifty-Four Squadron was scrambled several times on each of these days with the Luftwaffe launching heavy raids on Channel convoys and the south coast ports between Dover and Plymouth.

On each of these two days, the Luftwaffe suffered eighteen losses to the RAF's seven and five, respectively.

Finlay's delegation of responsibility worked—the flight shot down several German bombers—getting in so close that at the after action debriefing, his flight reported seeing the German crews so badly shot up that they could not bale out. They crashed into the Channel.

Finlay, the Olympic silver medalist was well pleased—his men had been bloodied and they had fought off the fighter escorts with the rest of 54 Squadron.

August came with some respite, and a short leave for his flight in late July. On August 8, 11, 12, 13, and 14, there was intense aerial combat. On these five days, the respective German losses to RAF losses were: 31:20, 38:32, 31:22, 45:13, and 19:8. The battle was intensifying. At Eleven Group Headquarters, Air Vice Marshal Keith Park and his commander in chief at Bentley Priory, Air Chief Marshal Sir Hugh Dowding, knew one key factor—the ratio had to be high in favor of the RAF because the Nazis had a large reserve of aircraft. They had yet to commit their full force. Goering was waiting, assessing, plotting—that was the RAF air intelligence assessment. They were correct.

Goering was about to launch "Adlertag" against the Royal Air Force on the ground—mass attacks on the RAF's bases, planning thereby to cripple the logistics of the RAF—fuel supplies, repair and maintenance facilities, hangars and storage, together with key structures, defensive systems, and most of all, aircraft on the ground. The plan called for overwhelming numbers—concentration of force—Goering knew this key, simple, and lethal principle of war. The Nazi Air Force chief's objective was to destroy RAF morale by wholesale bombing of all RAF station facilities—mess halls, accommodation huts, hospitals, and social facilities. He wanted Eleven Group's infrastructure destroyed.

August 15 and 16 witnessed the heaviest fighting so far in the battle. Many of Eleven Group's stations were subjected to heavy bomber raids. Damage was serious. In the air, the ratios on these days were 75:34 and 45:21 in favor of the RAF, but the damage on the ground was taking its toll.

Goering now intensified his ground attack plans, informing Hitler that all was on track for the invasion of Britain in September.

The weather then gave the RAF a welcome respite. On August 24, the weather improved and the Luftwaffe attacked with a vengeance. Finlay's station at Hornchurch was attacked with losses. The ratio was 38:22, much too close for Dowding and Park. Aircraft could not be replaced this quickly and, much more important, pilots were not only coming out of training at a slower rate than the losses, the new pilots were so inexperienced that they were going to front line squadrons with minimal hours in either Spitfires or Hurricanes.

The last days of August, from the 25 onward, constitutes six days of perilous attacks on RAF fields. The period to September 6 is when the RAF was at is most critical, from the commencement of Adlertag on August 13.

Finlay and his men were near exhaustion—constant sorties, no rest except for the lull caused by the poor weather, and the inevitable losses within 54 Squadron both in the air and on the ground. Airmen on the ground were now just as vulnerable as pilots aloft. Finlay's flight had performed superbly. He had led through the most intense aerial combat of the battle.

On September 7, two events happen to both 54 Squadron and the Eleven Group as a whole. The Germans switch to intensive day and night bombing of London. One thousand German aircraft were over London by day and night on September 7, causing massive damage to the London docks and the civilian population was hit badly. Eleven Group must fight now by day and by night, and 54 Squadron was now scrambling aircraft at a rate that was unsustainable. However, as Finlay pointed out in the officers' mess to his flight—"Thank God Gerry has shifted his attention to London and the cities, it takes the heat off our air fields; we can regroup on the ground, men. If they keep this up, this will be the biggest mistake that Goering and Hitler have made."

Finlay's words were prophetic. Dowding and Park had time to repair the fields and get damaged aircraft repaired.

The other event that occurred that put Finlay in the limelight, together with his squadron commander and the Hornchurch Station commander, was a surprise visit by Park himself to Hornchurch. He had made several other visits, flying in his own personal Hurricane. Today was different.

"So what went wrong?" Park said, looking Finlay's squadron commander in the eye, and also looking at Finlay for a possible answer.

"Very simple, sir," said the wing commander with a DFC and Bar, "Twelve

Group didn't turn up on time."

"What do you mean, exactly, 'didn't turn up on time,' the controllers at fighter command and our own people at Uxbridge watched the whole thing build up on radar as the enemy formed up to attack London. It was as clear as anything what was happening. We had them on radar all the way in. It was a simple vectoring job. It should have been a turkey shoot for God sake, Wing Commander. Tell me more. What's your interpretation of why London was hammered, and we were not there in sufficient force to prevent it. The prime minister is all over the C-in-C, ranting about incompetence and where were our squadrons when they were needed to defend London. Tell me, I'm all ears."

"Sir, all our squadron was airborne, like greased lighting. We had some aircraft that were hardly serviceable, but our men know what's going on with the poor devils on the ground in London, so every pilot that could fly and every aircraft that could get off the ground sortied, sir."

"So, what happened?" Park interjected.

"Well, to not put too fine a point on it we all got over London pronto, took down as many Gerry aircraft as we could, and then were running out of fuel. At this point, we expected the controllers to be handing off to Twelve Group, and all of their aircraft should have joined us over London when we were all running out of juice—aircraft from Duxford, Coltishall, Wittering, Digby, Kirton-in-Lindsey, and Church Fenton, were nowhere to be seen. They just never materialized. When we all landed again to refuel and go back into the fray, we were told that Gerry had 'beat a retreat' and that Twelve Group had appeared, belatedly, and were chasing some of the aircraft back toward Germany."

"I see…I see…." Air Vice Marshal Park paused, choosing his words carefully, he then asked. "So, why…why did this happen, Finlay, what's your assessment? You and your flight have seen more action than most. What happened?"

"I won't mince words, sir, it's Twelve Group's 'Big Wing Theory'—their idea of massing aircraft up north of London and then coming south in force to hammer the enemy. Sounds good in theory, but even on paper, it doesn't work."

"Why the hell not?" Park said in a very brusque, direct way.

"Simple, sir—speed, time, and distance—by the time Twelve Group gets airborne, assembles, and then moves in formation to the south, Gerry has done the damage and is off back home, mainly unaffected by Twelve Group. Meanwhile, my squadron, sorry…the wing commander's squadron, and the rest of the stations in Eleven Group that are scrambled, just do not have the numbers to take on Gerry when he flies 1,000 bomber raids. Worse still, by the time we've bloodied a lot of them, and we've got a lot, sir, we run low on fuel."

"And, if I can add to what Finlay said, sir, if we hold back aircraft until the first wave returns to refuel, we then find that we do not have enough aircraft overhead London to make a big dent on the enemy."

"Oh, my God!" said Park.

Everyone in the room waited for Park's next comments.

Then, for the first time that anyone could ever recall Park coming close to making an indiscrete comment for a group commander, he said, "Leigh-Mallory, the mighty 'Big Wing Theory' of Trafford Leigh-Mallory. Oh, have we paid dearly."

"Why didn't Headquarters just tell them to get their act south ASAP?" This comment came from an RAF Reserve pilot, in fact one of Roland Wells' trainees, a lawyer in civilian life, and a barrister.

"Now who are you, young man?"

"Flying Officer Toby Richardson, sir. You kindly signed my DFC citation." The regular Air Force officers cringed.

But Park did not get upset. "You've done some great flying Richardson, I'm proud of you. Yes, you are absolutely quite right. They were told to get south pronto. Think that Leigh-Mallory in his ivory tower up at Watnall just didn't get the big picture."

"Can we help further, sir? asked the station commander. Do you have any recommendations for us to improve our act here at Hornchurch?"

"No, good God, no; you've done a magnificent job. Well done all of you. The C-in-C is well pleased with all the Hornchurch squadrons."

He paused, raising his right hand to his chin in contemplation. "Okay. What's the time? What time is sunset? Please," said Park.

The answers were provided.

"I'll grab a quick sandwich; fuel up my aircraft soonest, please, call Twelve Group and let the good Air Vice Marshal Leigh-Mallory know that I'm on the way to see him."

"Yes, sir, right away."

"It's a courtesy call; tell his chief of staff that it's informal—no ballyhoo, please. I'm wearing my overalls, for goodness sake."

"Sir, I'm not being critical or anything," said Finlay, "but would you like me to fly you up in one of the trainers, save you the energy and worry of flying with everything else on your mind."

"Finlay, I'll accept that kind offer in the gracious spirit that I know it was given, but there's life in the old dog, yet. I'll fly myself."

They all laughed.

Finlay responded, "Yes, sir."

No sooner than Park had got airborne toward Nottinghamshire than the chins were wagging and the phones were ringing around the stations and squadrons.

The message was simple, Park versus Leigh-Mallory. How many rounds? No one could tell. Park was a fighter.

Finlay was about to get some welcome shuteye, when his batman informed him that there was a call for him in the mess.

"Roland, how the hell are you, where are you, what's up?" said Finlay.

"I'm working all the hours that God sends keeping Coventry Gear functioning."

"Good man, Roland. How's your girlfriend? Still okay, I hope.

"Absolutely! She's just fine. Look, Don, I want to get into the fight, for real. Weekend instructing at Oxford is not my idea of what a trained fighter pilot should be doing. My dad keeps me pretty well tethered to Coventry Gear. How about pulling a few strings with your squadron commander up to the group; tell them that you have a pilot wasted and kicking his heels here in Coventry."

"I have zero clout, Roland, with the people at Uxbridge, and I've set foot inside Bentley Priory once and that was to pick up my gong from the C-in-C."

"Sure you're sure?"

"Look, let me talk with my boss. He's close to the station commander who has a serious "in" with Park—they know each other well. That might work. I've got to get some shuteye, Roland. I'm knackered. London just took a beating again and we have been flying 'round the clock in the daylight hours. I promise you I'll do my best."

"Thanks, Don. Knew you'd help."

"Can't promise a thing, but I do know one thing, we are not just short of pilots, well...I'd better watch what I say, but...well...the real battle is about to take place—them or us. We need all the help we can get, Roland."

"Be careful, Don, no barrel rolls unless necessary, and watch your rear."

"I will, so long..." Finlay put the phone down and went to get some much deserved sleep.

Two days later, the chief of staff to the commander in chief fighter command at Bentley Priory asked his executive assistant to call Air Vice Marshal Park at Eleven Group.

Park took the call. "Sir, the chief of staff wants to talk with you, please; stand by."

"Wait a minute, what's it about, any idea?"

"I think your visit to see Twelve Group and your meeting with Air Vice Marshal Leigh-Mallory."

"I see, put him on, please; I'm all ears."

"Keith, good morning. Look, sorry to bother you when you've got your hands full, but we picked up on your meeting with Trafford Leigh-Mallory, or maybe I should say contretemps. I don't know whether that's a fair description, but the word got down to us, and now the C-in-C wants to know what's going on. I assume you two are at loggerheads over various things, am I correct?"

"Well, sir, that's not too far off the mark. I flew up to see Trafford after the mess that occurred over London the other day—you saw the damage reports and Goering's losses—not quite good enough for us at Eleven Group after what they did to London. My station commanders and squadrons were livid. I wanted to..."

Before he could go further, the chief of staff interrupted. "Keith, you know the drill. If there's a problem like this, bring it to us, that's why we have a staff—to resolve issues and make improvements—and, by the way...."

"Sir, I know that. This was about solving the problem at Leigh-Mallory's and my level, not running this up the flagpole and making it a major issue—not how I tend to do business, and so when we met..."

"Yes, when you met, you ran into Twelve Group flak, right? And Leigh-Mallory went on the defensive and told you were way out of line criticizing his 'Big Wing' tactics. Well, he called everyone that he knows that supports him, and bad mouthed you to everyone in the Air Ministry. That's how the C-in-C and I found out. Let me finish, Keith, I need to tell you something that you may not know and, if you do, you're forgetting. I'm your friend, Keith, so is the C-in-C. We think the world of you, that's why we put you in charge of Eleven Group, not Leigh-Mallory. However, he's got serious supporters in the Ministry and Whitehall—the up-and-coming crowd thinks that he walks on water, and you're one of Dowding's cronies. Nothing could be further from the truth, but it's the reality, Keith; remember perception is reality, the truth is often nowhere to be seen."

"I see, so he called people after we met."

"You bet he did."

"Well, I know where he stands now. Watch out for the next big disaster as Goering builds up over London. Churchill will not be pleased."

"He isn't already. The C-in-C took a roasting over the failures the other day. The PM ranted at him over the phone. It was ugly. Keith, the current chief of the air staff's days are numbered. Air Chief Marshal Newall's on the way out…keep that quiet, please, and he's a big supporter of yours and my boss, and therefore, by association, me. We can all go down together if the wrong people take over when Newall is retired. The Whitehall rumor mill is saying that he will be gone once the current crisis is over, assuming it is over, and he'll be retired to some far away colonial retirement position—New Zealand is the buzz."

"Oh, my God," uttered Park.

"Yes, you have it, so when you went up to see Leigh-Mallory and thought that you would give him a little private blasting and a lecture on aerial tactics, you walked into a hornet's nest, some may say a rats' nest. By the way, this is all strictly off line; you'd better not quote me on any of this, Keith, I can trust you?"

"Not a word. What a mess, just when the enemy is about to launch their biggest attacks ever. The next two weeks will be critical. If we cannot break them, we are in deep trouble."

"Exactly, Keith, and the last thing we want is Leigh-Mallory stirring the pot in London, and the C-in-C getting more abuse from the Prime Minister. What we want to do is the following—we'll call you both in, and the boss will play totally impartial referee—no sides—hear you both out, and then we'll promulgate new tactical obstructions ASAP after that meeting. We'll call you in about one hour. Stand by to get over here soonest. Working dress, the boss will be dressed up, the P.M.'s due out later—he wants answers for Winston. Got the picture, Keith?"

"Yes, sir, I do indeed."

"Remember who your friends are, Keith. We put you there. You're doing an outstanding job, and we don't want the apple cart rocked in the middle of this battle. Play it cool when you're with the C-in-C, and for goodness sake, don't get angry with Leigh-Mallory—be your usual highly professional self."

"Roger, sir. I'll be there soonest. I have several things to go over with the staff, in any case, regarding new pilots."

"Okay, Keith, we'll figure this out. You're a good man with a great future; don't ruin it because of a fight with a man who doesn't play by the rules. Not worth it, Keith."

"Thanks for the great advice, as always."

"Very good, Keith, get over here in plenty of time so that you can do your other things and be ready to meet with the C-in-C. Dowding will be his usual very straightforward self. Got it?"

"Got it."

"Out here, Keith."

"Goodbye, sir."

Three hours later, in his office at Bentley Priory, Air Chief Marshal Sir Hugh Dowding, commander-in-chief, fighter command, played the deftest hand of his military career, behind closed doors, with just three other men—his chief of staff, Park, and Leigh-Mallory. The outcome was to contribute significantly to the outcome of the battle.

He did not take sides in the great debate over the merits or otherwise of Leigh-Mallory's 'Big Wing' theory. He laid out tactical requirements based on operational realities, and then told them to go away and implement these realities immediately.

What he said was tactically critical for Britain's survival.

"It's all about speed, time, and distance; the timing of our first radar intercepts and the time it takes to determine the enemy's strengths, their various courses, air speeds to the most likely targets, and the estimates of their ETAs at various critical way points. Let me spell this out for you both. This is what I want."

Dowding stood up and went over to his huge wall chart.

"Look, gentlemen, we know the key vectors of the enemy. We plot them. What we, rather you two, have to do, no, must do, is get airborne in time to intercept at a time and place of 'our' choosing. When we attack, it will be knowing that they have neither unleashed their bombs, nor do they have reserves of fuel to go much further until the best estimated drop points—the target. You two must work together, you must get airborne to meet the enemy at these key way points that I have described, and in sufficient numbers to defeat the bombers and also take care of the fighter escorts. It's called maximum effort based on well thought through tactical application of the radar data and computation of these various key enemy parameters and way points. We meet them at their weakest moment, and then we attack them. Do you both understand what I expect now from both your groups? If we do this right, we will have the element of surprise with overwhelming force. But, and this is my concern, we will have little or no reserves to defend our air fields if they attack both the cities and the airfields simultaneously. Intelligence says no. They will concentrate most of their assets on the cities, and primarily London, for the next few weeks. I pray that they are correct. My very worst fear is that they send powerful dive bomber forces with fighter escorts to attack our airfields while we are up going after their bombers. Worst case is they find us on the ground, refueling—that is my single worst fear, gentlemen. Don't let it happen."

Dowding returned to his seat, and then looked both men squarely in the eyes. "Any questions?"

"No, sir."

"No, sir."

"Good. Make it happen, and immediately; work with the staff here and let me have the coordinated tactical plans by sunset today. Every day will be different. Every attack will vary, but it's our overall plan, this key tactical approach, that is so critical. Go to it. Good luck."

Park and Leigh-Mallory were temporarily joined in a common goal—to obey the commander in chief and implement his orders. The orders were unambiguous and totally rational. The facts spoke for themselves. There was no longer time for private theorizing.

The staffs at Bentley Prior, Uxbridge, and Watnall rolled up their sleeves.

Just as he was leaving, one of the Bently Priory personnel planners buttonholed Park.

"Got a minute, sir? Very brief, it's about a fellow called Wells, reserve Spitfire pilot, damn good instructor pilot training the new pilots. Shall we call him forward for front line service, sir? We're terribly short of experienced pilots, given our losses. Group said you know this man."

Park paused, and thought for several moments.

"No, we need him training. That's his job, and also he's needed back in Coventry making sure that we have something to fly when we lose aircraft. That's my decision."

"Yes, sir, very good."

Park left for Uxbridge in his staff car, and then, after a short break with his staff, took his personal Hurricane for a tour of each of his stations and a pep talk to all his station and squadron commanders, and pilots.

Dowding's plans were implemented. In effect, they were plans that Park had been using throughout the battle so far. Dowding knew this, and his chief of staff and Park knew this. Park never said a word.

The Luftwaffe attacked with unremitting force. Airfields at Croydon, Gosport, Ford, and Thorney Island were brutally attacked. Kenley airfield took a particularly heavy pounding with severe ground casualties. Worse still, the key radar station at Poling was hit badly. That morning, as dawn approached, Finlay sat in the mess eating eggs and bacon, toast, and a cup of coffee. He had learned the hard way years ago that with long sorties to the fuel limits of the Spitfire, too much fluid intake was a bad idea…nothing worse than a bladder attack during a dogfight. "You don't need to be taking a pee with Gerry on your tail, men," he exhorted his flight when they were first formed. "It's bad enough when you see Gerry coming up your arse in your mirror and you're getting ready to pull a few Gs to get the bastard off your tail, and you come out of a loop only to find that you need a change of underwear. One mug of coffee's enough, you'll have plenty of adrenalin to keep you high, trust me." The young pilots of 54 Squadron would laugh at Finlay's many and incisive tips that were subtle, or not so subtle, orders. They listened, for they rapidly learned that what Finlay imparted would without a shadow of doubt, save their lives.

Finlay had not had time to read his mail—two letters—one with a US postmark, and the other from the UK. Now was the time to catch up over breakfast.

Jesse Owens, Roland, and Don had written to each other continuously since their parting in Berlin in the summer of 1936. They were constantly in touch. The two British athletes were horrified to read that, on his return to the USA, Jesse had not been honored by America's leadership. "Hitler didn't snub me—it was FDR who snubbed me. The President didn't even send me a telegram," Jesse reported. "He hasn't invited me to the White House like so many other successful American athletes."

Roland and Don were horrified—one of the greatest athletes of all time, snubbed by his president, a so-called 'liberal' in British parlance. Finlay and Wells loved to exchange running notes with Owens.

Jesse would give them advice from across the Atlantic, "I let my feet spend as little time on the ground as possible—from the air, fast down, and from the ground, fast up."

They loved his comments and kept every letter in safe keeping. Worst of it all, Jesse reported to his British friends that he had, perhaps mistakenly in hindsight, ended his amateur status by taking up commercial offers that revolved around his running prowess and reputation. The American athletes association punished him by withdrawing his amateur status, thus, effectively ending his running career for all time. When war opened in Europe, Jesse was scrambling in a different way from Don Finlay in 54 Squadron—he was finding it increasingly hard to make a decent living, such was the status of a black person, and arguably the greatest athlete ever (perhaps with Carl Lewis in the 1984 Olympics).

Jesse had received letters from Germans who admired him, in direct contravention of Hitler's propaganda ministry's instructions. One German writer, a lawyer from Freiburg and a competitor in the 1936 Games, and a huge fan of Jesse Owens, sent him apologetic letters about his countrymen's attitudes. In one letter, he wrote about what Albert Speer, Hitler's architect for war production and armaments minister said about Jesse. He quoted in one letter what had been said by the Nazi leadership about Owens and African Americans:

"Each of the German victories, and there were a surprising number of these, made him happy, but he (Hitler) was highly annoyed by the series of triumphs by the marvelous colored American runner, Jesse Owens. 'People whose antecedents came from the jungle were primitive,' Hitler said with a shrug, 'their physiques were stronger than those of the civilized whites, and, hence, should be excluded from future games.'"

Roland Wells and Don Finlay could not help but privately ruminate on the fact that the American President had treated Jesse no better, in fact, he had been totally ignored. They were both horrified that he was not honored in his own country.

As Don Finlay put Jesse's letter back in its envelope, he looked at the next letter.

It was not good news, at least from the author's perspective. Roland had been officially denied the right of a full-time commission in the regular Air Force as a fighter pilot. He was instructed by Air Ministry directive to remain in the Reserves as an instructor pilot, though he was given the additional role and authority as an acting flight lieutenant, Royal Air Force Volunteer Reserve, to train new pilots in aerial warfare, as well as instruction on both the Spitfire and the Hurricane for which aircraft he was instructor qualified. Roland noted to Don that at least he could now get up in the air and teach his students how to engage the two twenty-millimeter cannons and four .303-millimeter machine guns. At least this way he felt that he joined the fray. The rest of the time, Roland noted, was spent back in Coventry with endless eighteen hours days spent with 'round-the-clock maximum effort at Coventry Gear's war production factory.

Before Finlay could down his coffee, the scramble alarms sounded. Fifty-Four Squadron was to get airborne immediately. They had not even been put on prior alert.

On August 18, the ratio of losses, in favor of the RAF, was 71:27.

Number 54 Squadron accounted for the demise of a good number of both Luftwaffe bombers and fighters.

The fighting intensified day by day, with breaks only caused by poor weather conditions that kept the Nazis on the ground in France.

On August 26, the ratio was 41:31, far too close a margin for Park's likes. The RAF was taking unacceptable losses. On this day, the Luftwaffe attacked Dover and Folkestone, 54 Squadron's station at Hornchurch, and the large Portsmouth naval base. At night the Nazis attacked Plymouth naval base, and also the industrial heartland in the Midlands, with attacks on Birmingham, and…Coventry.

During the August 26 raid on Coventry, Roland's impressive training of his workmen in firefighting and damage control, together with supplemental first aid training, paid off. The factory was spared any direct hits, but surrounding businesses and residences were hit. There were a number of civilian casualties. Coventry Gear auxiliaries helped fight the fires, recovering the dead from the ruined buildings, helping rescue trapped victims of the raid, and clearing the roads of debris. This was the shape of things to come. Coventry had been bloodied.

Roland now realized one essential thing, just as his father had predicted, he was now on the front line just as much as if he was in his Spitfire or Hurricane training his pilots straight out of basic flying training.

As the corpses were removed from surrounding devastated buildings by Coventry Gear men helping the Coventry fire brigade and ambulance service, he knew one thing—it would get a lot worse before it would get better. He had fore-bodings. Frederick Wells told his son to spend more time training the men on the use of all the firefighting equipment and first aid appliances.

"Roland, this is the beginning, Son; the bastards are going to come after all the major industrial centers, mark my words. Let's get the air raid shelters improved with additional sand bags, please, and by the way, let's go underground too—dig underground bunkers. At least this will help mitigate lateral blast and heat effects. If there's a direct hit…well, nothing will save us."

"Will do, Dad, right away. By the way, I'm installing additional air raid sirens. With all the noise in some of the workshops, the outside sirens in the city are difficult to hear at first. As soon as the city sirens sound, we'll sound our own, too, in the workshops."

"Good job, Son. Terrific!"

Frederick paused, clearly worried about something else.

"What's up, Dad?"

"It's your mother; she's volunteered to drive an ambulance. She's a damn good driver, that's the problem, but it worries me to death if anything happens to her."

"Dad, you said it to the men the other day when you addressed them; we're all in it together. She wants to do her bit like the rest of us."

"I know, God bless her, but…well, I can't stop worrying about her in the middle of the night with no lights because of the blackout, weaving through our city streets with bombs falling all around her."

"Dad, that's what she wants to do."

Roland paused, because he could see that his father was visibly distressed.

"Dad, I haven't said this to you, and I want to say something. I'm glad that I'm here with you, doing our bit for the war effort. I'm so proud of you." He put his arm around his father, and for a few brief and highly emotional moments, farther and son shared a precious father-son moment.

Since Adlertag on August 13, Goering's air force hit the RAF's Eleven Group's stations whenever weather permitted. The group was on the ragged edge. Park worked twenty-hour days, getting cat naps between actions in his operations center and flying between stations, often in the middle of intensive aerial combat overhead.

As the first week of September ended, Park and Dowding reviewed the situation at Bentley Priory.

As both men watched the battle progressing from the position above the fighter command HQ operations room, both Park and Dowding looked at each other.

"My God, Keith," Dowding exclaimed. "They've changed their targets. They're going for the cities…London's now the target…they're leaving our airfields alone. They're massing to hit London. Keith, get ready for the biggest attack on London ever."

"Yes, sir."

"I think that Hitler and Goering have just made their first and biggest mistake of the war—by attacking our cities and leaving our airfields alone, they've given us the breathing space we need to regroup and get our airfields and aircraft back in shape. Thank God." Dowding took a deep breath, and smiled like he had never smiled in weeks since the battle began. He visibly strode like a man possessed from the operations center to his office—he wanted to impart the news to the other group commanders.

Hitler's reprisal on British cities for the accidental and indiscriminate attack on Berlin by RAF bomber command had, by a stroke of supreme good fortune, bought Dowding and Park the time they needed. This was now a decisive turning point. The Luftwaffe bomber fleets would be decimated by RAF fighter command as they attacked British cities and then tried to make the perilous return journey with fighter command harassing them all the way to the maximum range and endurance of the Spitfire and Hurricane Squadrons.

Goering pitted 1,000 aircraft against London by day, followed by intensive nighttime raids.

Finlay's Flight and 54 Squadron as a whole were at the limits of their endurance—sortie after sortie—with Finlay losing, inevitably, some of his pilots, both experienced and not so experienced. They were beginning to face overwhelming odds. Finlay reminded his men in their ready room of what the prime minister had said earlier, "We will never give up, and we will never surrender."

On September 15, 1940, the Luftwaffe mounted the largest ever attack on London, in two massive raids.

Twenty Four Squadrons of Fighter Command went into action this day. The Nazis suffered huge losses, suffering a loss ratio of 60:26. It was a massive and undisputed victory for the Royal Air Force.

Goering was furious.

In the mess at Hornchurch that night, exhausted crews drank a well earned beer, saddened by the losses that they had suffered, but exhilarated by their colossal victory. "Well," said Finlay to his men, "we showed the bastards what for; we never gave up and we never surrendered. Hitler and his thugs won't be marching down Whitehall any time soon."

Everyone in the Hornchurch mess raised their glasses and cheered.

Finlay left the mess and went to see his maintenance teams in the hangars to thank them, congratulate them for their sterling efforts, and to say, "Men, we've got them on the run. We're going to crack the Hun. Just hang in there, men, and we'll all see this one through together. Thank you for all you have done. Without you, our aircraft would not be up there taking care of those bastards."

On September 15, Finlay and his men slept the sleep of heroes.

September 15, 1940, would be known forever as, *"Battle of Britain Day."*

The Luftwaffe was defeated. By October 31, 1940, the Germans' hopes of invading Britain were over. The Battle of Britain was over—it was a total victory for those in the air, those who supported the aircrew, and the industrial base that provided the equipment.

Fifty-Four Squadron was moved for a rest to Number Thirteen Group, fighter command at Catterick, under the overall command of Air Vice Marshal Saul, headquartered at Newcastle upon Tyne. The squadron was highly decorated for its bravery and heroic efforts.

Finlay was wounded and then promoted to command Number 41 Squadron, Fighter Command. The following year in August 1941, he would be promoted to Wing Commander and was made the Group Engineering Officer of Eleven Group. In June 1942, Finlay would receive the Distinguished Flying Cross. During the Battle of Britain, Don Finlay shot down four enemy aircraft, shared two destroyed, three enemy aircraft badly damaged, and one shared badly damaged. Most of all, he led one of the deadliest flights of 54 Squadron, with a total enemy tally that was impressive.

Chapter Eleven
GLORY AND RETIREMENT

"I don't believe it," said Roland over the phone to Don Finlay. "What genius made these kinds of decisions, for goodness sake?"

"Well, the rumor is that Dowding ticked off Churchill too many times."

"How do you mean, he and Park saved the day, saved the country, saved the world, for God's sake."

"Preaching to the choir, Roland," commented Finlay. "Politics, and more politics, that's what this is all about. You're either in or you're out at that level."

"But I still don't quite understand why Dowding's being given the heave ho, into retirement of all things?"

"Simple, ever since he took a stand against Churchill before Dunkirk and refused, on pain of resignation I've been told by my new boss, that he would not commit any more fighter command squadrons to France because, if we did, we would be naked when the Nazis attacked Britain, Churchill's had it in for Dowding. Churchill's great, but I gather he cannot tolerate opposition, and particularly when they turn out to be right, as Dowding clearly was."

"I see, that explains a lot."

"It gets worse, Roland."

"You're kidding."

"No, I'm not, I wish I was. Evidently during the battle, Churchill would turn up at Bentley Priory and Park's Headquarters at Uxbridge and tell both of them how to run the battle. Dowding politely told Churchill on several occasions that he was in command, and when down at Uxbridge during the most intense fighting, Dowding supported his group commander to the point of telling Churchill that fighting and commanding had to be left to him and his Group commanders, and that political interference in the middle of the battle was not welcomed. Churchill evidently bristled, stalked off back to London, and made a mental note—clearly,

58

that Dowding was at the end of his career when the battle was over."

"Such is the reward for success."

"Worse still, Roland, Park got caught up in the flak, being a Dowding protégée and the key leader during the battle. His future is undetermined, as yet."

"I can't believe it. Park won the battle"

"Everyone knows it who knows anything, Roland, but tell that to all the new boys who have taken over in the Air Ministry in Whitehall. Leigh-Mallory is on the way up, and Park is either moving sideways or to some far away job. It's all politics, Roland, it stinks. Dowding is being retired. Poor devil has not even been elevated to marshal of the Royal Air Force, after all that he has done. He's being retired in his exiting rank, air chief marshal. What a disgrace."

"My dad will be horrified when he hears all this."

"Nothing anyone can do, decisions are made—Dowding is being retired, put out to pasture without so much as a peerage or anything, and Park, well, we'll see where he ends up. His dire rival, Leigh-Mallory, is the apparent winner of the promotions stakes. It's pretty disgusting."

"When you have some idea on your leave, come on down to Coventry, stay with my parents, see the factory, meet the men, and give everyone a little boost."

"I'd love to do that. I'll call you once I know when I've got four or five days off."

"Before we sign off, I heard from the States; Jesse is not doing well. Sounds like he's in financial trouble and is not recognized by the leadership. He should be honored as a national hero, made a leader to get them ready for what's inevitable—they're going to have to fight, sooner or later."

"Tell me about it," said Don. "They're in 'La-La land' over here. They have no idea. Only people like Ed Morrow know what it's like here. Thank God for people like him. At least Roosevelt had the guts to get rid of that Nazi-loving ambassador and replaced him with this great fellow, Winant. He's incredible—came to visit us at Hornchurch. I love the man, what an Anglophile. I've got to go, Roland."

"See you when you come down. Let me know once you know your leave dates. Out here, too."

Roland and Don put their phones down. Little did Don know, his great friend, fellow athlete, and pilot, was about to enter the fray in ways that no one, just no one, could ever have anticipated, and in the summer of 1936, in the balmy, sunlit streets of Berlin, envisage the tragedy that would unfold.

Chapter Twelve
NOVEMBER 14, 1940 - COVENTRY, ENGLAND
A NIGHT TO REMEMBER

In London, Winston Churchill faced one of the toughest and heart wrenching decisions of his life, the price of ultimate leadership, and the loneliness of one in the highest position of authority. He was about to pay the massive emotional price of being Britain's wartime leader.

Churchill went into the inner sanctum of the special security briefing room. A Royal Air Force wing commander was waiting to brief the prime minister. With him were two civilian analysts from Bletchley Park, on the outskirts of London. No one, except the tiny few who were briefed into the top secret special access program knew what went on in the huts surrounding the main building at Bletchley Park. It was in these huts that Britain's best brains used the Enigma machines captured from the Germans to break the Nazi codes and read their 'Top Secret' special communications. The special material was stamped, TOP SECRET, ULTRA, the codeword for Enigma decrypted information, the most prized, and the most secret intelligence of World War II. Those who were read into the Ultra program would have no future if they so much as even indicated the existence of such a program, let alone its substantive content.

Churchill was joined by the chief of the air staff, the chief of the general staff, the first sea lord, and the directors of naval and air force intelligence. The cabinet secretary handled the prime minister's personal copies of the latest intelligence and the assessments from the Bletchley Park analysts.

The news this day was momentous and the implications not just dire, but disturbing in ways that made Winston Churchill look frail, stressed, and full of foreboding.

The wing commander was precise and brief. "Prime Minister, sir, the intercepts show that the Luftwaffe is planning a massive attack tonight. The operation is called 'Moonlight Sonata' by the Nazis. Luftflotte number 3 will be the main instrument of the attack—515 German bombers will constitute the attacking force. Our problem is that we do not know the exact target. We have best estimates, but we cannot be absolutely sure. Our assessment is that it may well be Coventry. We know that their main goal is to destroy British industrial infrastructure—about 25 percent of all our main military aircraft are made in Coventry, together with other armaments, military vehicles, weapons, and aircraft engines that make Coventry a most probable target. We assess that if, and I stress 'if' Coventry is indeed their objective that no target in the city will be spared. It will be a mass aerial bombardment of the center of the city where most of the industry is located. We can also expect indiscriminate bombing if any of the aircraft are off their targets through poor navigation and loss of situational awareness. We have seen this on countless occasions when German bombers get lost."

"My God," said Churchill, "what is the probability, Wing Commander?"

"Sir, we just do not know the exact target. This is Bletchley's very best estimate. Now, unfortunately, sir, some further bad news."

"It gets worse?" asked Churchill.

"Afraid so, sir. The system that we use to track the German bomber force when it departs the various bases in German is down. It's currently inoperable. You may recall from an earlier briefing that this system intercepts the beams that the Germans use to guide or navigate their aircraft to British targets. We have been jamming these beams once intercepted. With much regret, sir, I have to report that it is inoperable as of now. Teams of technicians are working 'round the clock to repair it."

"I see. Is there anything else that I need to know?"

"The good news is that, although we cannot be sure of the exact target, we have Ultra intercepts from multiple communications sources. We know exactly which units from which bases will attack, and their attack plans—times of take-off, likely courses, altitudes, and their planned times to arrive over our coast. We know their sequencing and bomb loads. It will be an aerial flotilla—Reichsmarschall Goering at his very worst, I'm afraid, Prime Minister."

"What are they using?"

"The bad news, sir, is that their initial attack aircraft will use marker flares by their pathfinders, then high explosive bombs, followed by incendiaries to start fires and light up the targets, and then the heavy bombers will drop regular bombs on the order of 1,000 pounds. They mean to destroy the target area and leave nothing standing."

"Do we have any political intelligence associated with their planning?"

"Yes, sir. Hitler has made it clear to Goering that he wants to send a message to Britain that they intend to bring us to our knees, that no one will be spared, and that he expects the Luftwaffe to lose few aircraft in this major nighttime raid. Hitler has ordered an unremitting Blitzkrieg. If it is indeed Coventry, the most likely assessed target, Hitler wants Coventry destroyed."

Churchill turned to the chief of the air staff, "What can we do?"

"Sir, we are desperately working to increase the number of night fighters in the squadrons designated to defend the cities, but as of now we have just a handful of qualified aircraft and pilots. We are virtually totally reliant on anti-aircraft guns and barrage balloons for our defense. Our only other main defense is that they will have little time over Coventry given the distances involved, but if they light up the city finding the city center will not be difficult. Tonight the weather will be good. They will not be cloud protection for the city. I wish that I had better news, sir."

"Very well, we have to increase night fighter production and you have to get more and more pilots trained to fight at night. That has my highest priority. Now, to my biggest concerns and questions."

There was deathly hush in the room. What would Churchill say next? No one was about to preempt the Prime Minister.

"How critical is it to protect Enigma and the Ultra product?"

The chief of the air staff became the principal spokesman for the collective chiefs of staff.

"Sir, if we had the physical means to beat off this attack with sufficient night fighters and really blunt the Luftwaffe, we would advise that we do meet them as soon as they cross the coast and attack them all the way to Coventry and all the way back across the Channel until their own fighters join the fray. But, the sad fact is, sir, that we don't have the resources; we are simply unable to mount a sufficiently solid night counter-offensive. On a perfectly moonlit summer night we might be in better shape, but November is not that time of the year."

The day was November 14, 1940, a day that will live in the annals of British history.

Churchill lit a cigar and took a drink of water, and then cleared his throat.

"Gentlemen, we cannot compromise Enigma in these circumstances. The Germans will realize that we have some means of obtaining prior warning if we mount even the most meager counterattack as they cross our shores. We have to protect this source. We cannot, at this stage of the war, give up its huge benefits. Reading the Germans' mail and knowing their every move is critical. It is a war winning capability. If they change the Enigma machine for a new device, we will lose the most valuable intelligence asset that we will ever have. I cannot compromise that. There will be no defense except that we should go after them once they can reasonably expect us to have figured out the attack. I want you and your staffs to work that out, presumably as they depart the area and head back to Germany."

The group was stunned. The implications were horrendous for Coventry.

"Sir, what about the city?"

"What do you mean?"

"Well, shall we order an evacuation? Give the people time to get out of the city center before the attack? Have the fire services and medical teams standing by?"

This was now one of the toughest and most wrenching questions asked of Winston Churchill.

Churchill just paused. He puffed at his cigar, took more sips of water, and then...."No."

"No, sir?" asked the cabinet secretary.

"The answer's 'no,' we will not warn the city. Their intelligence people will easily find out that we had forewarning, and then they will realize we knew that they were attacking, and then the next question will be easy—how did the British know? Have they our codes?"

The room went completely silent. Churchill just stared at the wall chart with the details of the planned Luftwaffe attack on what was most likely to be Coventry, with markers for each of the German airfields, numbers of units, and their planned tracks to the British coast, with times of the way points and ETAs over the most likely targets, including Coventry. The intelligence was 100 percent accurate and in fine detail.

"That is my decision, gentlemen. Only I can make it. I am sorry that we have no choice. We cannot give up Enigma's enormous benefits. Meanwhile, let us intensify the production of night fighters and get a long range fighter on the drawing boards."

Churchill returned to his underground bunker. Tonight he would not sleep, not one wink, except perhaps to pass in and out of a comatose state as he envisaged what the night would bring to the citizens of the massive Luftwaffe attack, and their most likely destination, Coventry.

In Coventry, and at Coventry Gear, the night shift clocked in.

Frederick Wells left his office, and told his driver to find his son and tell him that it was time to go home.

It was just before 7 o'clock.

The city was in a state of complete blackout as his car made its way toward Keresley. The air raid wardens were on patrol, and City of Coventry policemen were checking cars' occupants. Frederick Wells' car went on its way unimpeded. His car began to reach the outskirts of the city.

Fredrick Wells turned to his son, "Hope that your mother has a quiet night. She's supposed to be back at midnight once they stand down the reserve ambulance crews. Do you know to pick her up from the hospital?" Frederick was addressing his driver.

"Yes, sir. Mrs. Wells and I chatted earlier in the day. We're good to go. I'll be at the hospital before midnight to pick her up, sir, don't worry. I'll get her home safely."

"Thank you," said the owner of Coventry Gear. He had no sooner finished his response when the sky behind them was suddenly lit up.

It was 7:20 P.M.

To the rear, the whole of the city was lit up by blazing lights followed by explosions. Wells ordered the car stopped. They got out and Roland said spontaneously, "My God, the city is being attacked. It's an air raid."

"Turn the car round; we're going back."

"Yes, sir."

By the time the car came to the edge of the inner- city area, the noise of high explosive detonations was deafening. Two policemen stopped the car.

"Sorry, sir, you cannot go further. There's an air raid on; it's big, you have to go back, and we cannot allow anyone back into the city. We need to keep all the roads clear for the fire brigade and ambulances. It's going to be bad, very bad, sir."

I'm Frederick Wells, the owner of Coventry Gear. I need to get to the factory. We have to help."

Sir, I know who you are, but with great respect, sir, we just cannot let you go into the city—look, sir, the whole place is being bombed. You must do as we say, sir. Stay with us if you like, but we may get bombed here, too. Those last bombs were a close call."

As the policeman finished his last words, a series of explosions almost lifted them all off their feet, the heat and blast was that intense, and Roland grabbed his father and told him to get down behind the rear of the car. All five men lay on the ground—hands over their ears—the noise was deafening.

Roland got up slightly and looked 'round the side of the car, kneeling rather than risking standing. Within seconds, the explosions were so intense one of the policeman said that they needed to retreat. The two policemen had bicycles.

"Everyone, get in the car, you two included," he shouted to the policemen. "If we stay here, we'll all be killed! I'll drive." The five men piled into the car.

Roland swung the car 'round and accelerated away from the edge of the city. Within seconds, the area where they had been waiting was obliterated by high explosive bombs, destroying all the surrounding buildings, and tearing up the road where the car had been parked.

"God, I hope that mum is okay." Roland accelerated down the road and into suburban Coventry. As they drove, the whole area was alight with incendiaries. The policemen asked to stop and get out once they reached what seemed like a safe place.

"This may not be safe either," said Roland.

"We have to stop traffic and keep control of movements," said the policeman. The two 'Bobbies' got out of the car. "Drive home, Roland, let me see if I can talk to the factory by phone."

"Keep your heads down," Roland called to the two policemen, as they stood in the middle of the road.

Roland's words were the last the two policemen would ever hear.

As Roland and his father drove away, they had gone no further than a half a mile when a 1,000-pound bomb exploded close to the policemen. A huge crater was left where the men stood, and the entire group of surrounding houses was severely damaged. People were screaming as the facades of row houses collapsed, leaving the insides of the building exposed like doll's houses. Floors inside collapsed, taking their residents with them.

As Roland reached the countryside, fire trucks from surrounding towns and villages were clanging their bells as they raced toward Coventry. When they reached the house Frederick ran inside, told the maid and cook to get down into the underground shelter in the garden, and he reached for the nearest phone. He frantically called several numbers at Coventry Gear…none of them answered.

In the city, fire hydrants were destroyed and the roads were becoming impassable with debris. Craters in the main roads made it difficult to traverse the roads. The main fire station in the center of the city took a direct hit. By now, fortunately, all the vehicles were out fighting the huge fires and attempting to rescue people who were trapped and calling from the debris of destroyed buildings. Within no time, there was no hydrant water. All the mains supplies were ruptured. The fires raged.

In the midst of the carnage and destruction, another wave of Luftflotte 3 arrived overhead and disgorged their bomb bays on the very center of Coventry.

At approximately 8 o'clock, the fourteenth-century St. Michael's cathedral took a direct hit from 1,000-pound bombs and incendiaries. Coping with the inferno inside the cathedral was impossible. The main roof collapsed and Coventry cathedral was destroyed, with the exception of the outer walls and spire.

The main Coventry and Warwickshire Hospital had not been hit. Power was lost and the doctors and nurses were frantically coping with emergency power generation.

Elizabeth Wells never faltered once in going out from the main ambulance station with her reserve ambulance, equipped only with the basic first aid gear. Her two male auxiliaries and one nurse hung on inside as she drove through the streets of Coventry, with bombs exploding nearby, and the light from the fires enabling her to see through the smoke from the fires. Her colleagues performed on the spot first aid for those they could help; for many, help could do little to save them. Their injuries were so massive that they had to be left in order to save those with some hope of surviving. The most severely injured of those that they assessed had some chance, were ferried to the hospital. The four-person crew of her ambulance would work through the night until they faced their final nemesis—there was no fuel left at the station to refuel the ambulance. They then resorted to waiting for casualties to be brought from the debris so that they could treat them. Any available vehicle was then commandeered to drive victims to the hospital. It was a matter of improvisation in a desperate situation.

At about midnight the "all clear" was sounded. The acrid smoke from the fires filled the rescuers' lungs, people already exhausted from five frantic hours of rescue work, and surrounded by death and destruction.

For all the rescue teams, they too were concerned for their loved ones and homes. What would they find when they returned to the streets where they lived? Some were so exhausted and stressed by the carnage and mutilation that they simply broke down. Elizabeth took a ride to the hospital to help. The wards were totally overcrowded, the calm efficiency of the doctors, nurses, and auxiliary helpers still shining through despite the tragedy that unfolded in the operating theaters and wards. The morgue could not cope and bodies were simply covered and stacked wherever there was space.

Elizabeth had little or no time to think about her own family and Coventry Gear, located not in the city center itself, but very close by. Reality soon hit, and it was the most traumatic experience of her life so far.

She was in the ward helping the nursing staff with casualties when she recognized one of the victims that had just been brought in—one of the foremen gear cutters from Coventry Gear.

She soothed him. He had multiple fractures—ribs, legs, and major head lacerations.

"Bert, what happened? How are the others?"

"The shops took a direct hit, Mrs. Wells. I was blown off my feet and came 'round with some firemen lifting me from the building; I think a lot of our men didn't make it, ma'am. All I could see were the remains of our workshop when they lifted me into the ambulance."

"Where are the others?"

"I don't know, Mrs. Wells; I don't know." His blackened face and bandaged head hid the tears streaming down his face from both the pain from his injuries and the sheer emotion of what he had experienced.

"It's okay, don't you worry; you're in good hands now. I'll leave you to the nurse while you wait for the doctor. I'll see if I can find any of the others."

Elizabeth walked the wards and saw several Coventry Gear men being treated, the night shift workers that had only just come on when the raid started.

She then found one of the senior air raid wardens, who was one of the gate staff at Coventry Gear.

"How's the factory?"

"Not good, ma'am. Three of the shops took direct hits. I think...well, I think," he paused, "there's a lot of dead and injured. Thank God your husband and young Mr. Wells had gone for the evening and did not stay on to work."

Elizabeth almost collapsed with this news, thankful for their survival, and now totally exhausted. Her energy now left her. The adrenalin had all but gone. She had nothing left to give.

"Here's a cup of tea," said one of the WVS workers. She recognized Mrs. Wells. "You've given a lot, just drink this; it will buck you up a little."

By two in the morning, Elizabeth came out of her daze and returned to the wards to help.

Back at the Wells' family home, Frederick and Roland were beside themselves with worry. They had also been very lucky. The Germans had, in retrospect, clearly been trying to find the 'shadow factory' that produced armaments a few miles away in Brown's Lane, well on the outskirts of the city where, in peacetime, Jaguar cars were manufactured. The Germans had been unsuccessful and their bomber crews had indiscriminately discharged their bombs, destroying homes in the suburbs, and killing many innocent people who had been caught unawares and had no shelters to hide in underground. Two 1,000-pounders exploded in the field behind the main garden to Frederick Wells' residence. The blast shook the house, cracking the rear façade and blew out the windows. Both men had been extremely lucky. They had not taken shelter, believing they were secure so far from the city.

"Let's get in the car, Roland. We have to find your mother and see what has happened to the factory."

Roland drove.

It was the most stressful drive that either man would ever take. Driving from the countryside into the suburbs, they were horrified at what they saw even several miles from the city center. Whole rows of houses had been destroyed where the Luftwaffe had dropped their bombs indiscriminately. People were frantically searching through the debris. Fires were uncontrollable. There were not enough fire engines and ambulances. As they slowly moved along the cratered roads into city, the reality of the attack became a nightmare.

The city center of Coventry was destroyed. They could see the outer shell of the cathedral with smoke rising from the debris. As they approached the hospital, Frederick simply said, "Thank God." The hospital had not been hit. "What a miracle!"

They parked beside a convoy of ambulances and open trucks that had brought in the dead and injured. Inside they wandered the wards, in desperation, when Frederick's arm was touched by one of the WVS volunteers.

"Mr. Wells, sir, your wife's in one of the back wards, helping the nurses prepare casualties for surgery."

Frederick simply stood there, transfixed, just staring into the lady's face, her ruddy complexion and stained uniform transfixing him.

Her words said one thing—his wife was alive.

He said two simple words, several times, "Thank you, thank you...thank you."

Roland and his father entered the surgical area, and there, helping several nurses tend to a casualty who was being anesthetized, was his beloved wife.

Roland touched his father's arm.

"I think she's busy, Dad."

Once the patient was wheeled into the operating theater, Fredrick embraced his wife; it was the embrace of a lifetime.

On the night of November 14, 1940, 600 people died in what became known as 'The Great Raid on Coventry,' and over 1,000 were injured. Over 4,000 homes were destroyed. The center of the city was all but obliterated. The Nazis, in their own inimitable and evil way, conjured up the most diabolic and macabre description to encapsulate what they had done to the people of Coventry and their beautiful medieval city, 'To Coventrate.'

Frederick and Roland Wells had to endure several hours of intense frustration, until after first light, before the air raid wardens and the bomb disposal experts would declare the area that led to Coventry Gear safe for transit. There was a serious and real fear of unexploded bombs. Several had been located. More were believed to be lodged in the debris.

Over a mug of tea on the hospital grounds, Frederick said to his son, "Tonight, Son, our great city has taken the most appalling and devastating beating that will live forever in the annals of tyranny." He then paused, "But Hitler will reap the whirlwind, and the German people will pay for these atrocities in ways the likes of which the world has never seen."

Roland looked at his father. He could see that his father—a kind, caring, and loving man—was now in a different mode. When he said that Hitler would reap the whirlwind, he knew that his father was predicting events that he could not conceive as a younger man.

When they arrived at the main gate of Coventry Gear, both men had psychologically conditioned themselves for the worst. They were very wise to have done this.

Three shops were totally destroyed to the point of being shells; others had suffered blast and heat damage, but would be operational. The other operational impacts were self evident—there was no power, no water, and, naturally, no communications. The worst was to follow.

When they reached the hardest hit area inside the factory compound, the senior air raid warden escorting Frederick Wells prepared him for the shock ahead. There had not been time to move the corpses of the dead. They were laid out with covers over them, the simplest tarpaulins.

Tears welled in both men's eyes. Frederick Wells pulled himself together. "How many?"

"I'm very sorry, sir, you've lost about 80 of your men. They died instantly from direct hits. Now, for the worst part that I have to tell you, Mr. Wells…"

Frederick stared at him, it being inconceivable that there could be worse news.

"Well, sir, we've done a numbers tally. The dead here are those whose bodies we could recover, and were in state to be recovered. I have to tell you we know that some of your men were simply obliterated in the far shop—looks like two 1,000-pounders went straight into the main area. I'm sorry to say, well, there was very little that we could find of several of your workers' remains. It's pretty bad, sir."

"I see."

"We are still searching for remains in that shop. There's nothing that we can identify—no person, sir, just parts. It's awful. We have a few people in there now. It's gruesome work."

"Let me go with you. I want to talk to these people."

As they walked through the factory toward the worst hit area, Wells asked the senior warden about names, whether their families had been informed, and so on.

"No, sir. None of this has been done. It's 9 o'clock; we're all exhausted."

"Let me try to find the night shift rosters in the office. Thank God, that's still standing; otherwise, we wouldn't know who was on last night.

The rest of November 15 and for several days afterwards, Frederick Wells had to endure with his son the terrible duty of informing and visiting the families of the dead workers. Even more tragedy was heaped on tragedy. The homes of many of the dead had been destroyed, too. In several, cases, whole families had been lost. The tragedy of it all was overwhelming.

The inner strength and leadership of the Coventry Gear team came through. Once power, lighting, and water were restored, they set about getting the factory back into production. Amidst the longest days of constant work, Frederick Wells had to host VIP visits, the media, the insurers, and people from the Ministry of Aircraft Production in London. He ensured that his people were fed as much as they could be, given the already difficult food rationing. His wife and the wives of his managers and senior foremen worked the saddest tasks of all—consoling, comforting, and helping in a multiplicity of ways—the widows and families of the dead men.

Frederick Wells would not say this to his work force at the all hands type addresses he would deliver to rally his people and maintain morale, but he was inwardly stressed by the thought that the Nazis would attack again.

His worst fears were, in fact, correct; but, mercifully, the Germans did not attack again in 1940. Coventry Gear had rebuilt itself when the next attacks occurred on April 8 and 9, 1941, April 10 and 11, 1941, and the last raid on Coventry on August 3, 1942.

At a banquet dinner in Coventry, Wells was the guest speaker in early 1943 to reflect on how Coventry had survived, had come through, would rebuild, and would go onwards and upwards, as he termed it. He reminded his audience that Coventry had lost 1,250 of its citizens in the raids. His voice was full of emotion when he praised the citizens of Coventry for their courage, fortitude, and determination to not give up. He committed himself, and he felt sure that he spoke for all citizens of this great city, when he concluded that the war would be won, Hitler would be brought down, and the city would emerge from the war to rebuild itself in the spirit that had enabled it to survive the ultimate test of survival.

The applause was stunning. Everyone in the banquet hall stood, and clapped, and clapped…and clapped.

Chapter Thirteen
JESSE BIRKETT'S WAR

Roland and Jesse became inseparable after November 14, 1940. The frailty of life became more and more apparent as the war entered 1942, with the entry of the United States into the war following the December 7, 1941 attacks by the Japanese on the United States Pacific Fleet at Pearl Harbor in the Hawaiian Islands.

Jesse had done all she could to play her part in rebuilding Coventry Gear after the 'Great Raid.' Her special work for the technical intelligence community had wound down after she had updated the documentation on the various German systems. Her language skills were becoming rusty.

She was leaving the hangar out at Coventry Airport on a cold and very miserable, late February day in 1942 to meet Roland for lunch when a man appeared in her office, a man whom she had never seen before. He was dressed in very smart attire at a time when clothing was short in supply and people made do with whatever they had at the beginning of the war.

"Ms. Birkett, I presume?" the man began.

"Yes, I'm Jesse Birkett. What can I do for you? I don't recall having an appointment with anyone today. Did you call?"

"No, I did not call. Here is my identification."

He produced a photo ID card with an embossed Royal Crown and an insignia indicating that he was a special investigator with the war office.

"Okay, what can I do for you? I'm in a bit of a hurry; I'm supposed to meet my boyfriend for lunch at 12:30 in the Golden Cross Pub in town."

"I know. I was at Coventry Gear earlier. I've been interviewing some people there about you. I met your boyfriend, Mr. Wells. Very nice young man, Reserve pilot, and a chip off the old block, just like his dad. We love Freddie Wells in London."

"Interviewing people about me…what for, may I ask? Who are you really?"

"Look, nothing to worry about; by the way, I suggested to Mr. Wells that he meet you at one o'clock. This won't take long; just an initial meeting. Look, Miss Birkett, Jesse; May I call you Jesse, please?"

"Everyone else does, go ahead…please."

"You're a very talented lady. People in London that I work with liked the fine work that you did on the engines project. Great job! You've got some serious language skills, French and German."

"You seem to know a lot."

"That's my job. We'd like to use your talents more. As far as I am concerned, you're ideal for some other work, very important work. Everyone who knows you trusts you, and you are extremely discreet and most trustworthy. Not a bad word said about you by anyone. Key thing is, the people you worked for on the project really thought so highly of you, they thought that you shouldn't be wasted."

"I see."

"Look, you want to get off to lunch. That's fine. What I would like to do is to invite you down to London to meet some people, people that you haven't met before. Interesting people; you'll like them. Very important work. Here's a travel warrant to London and return. When can you come down; sooner the better if you can, please?"

He was polite, respectful, and quite gentlemanly.

Jesse was intrigued, could hardly refuse, and said yes, but she would have to get permission for a day off.

"Already arranged…no problem. The big boss said yes, anytime. Mr. Wells senior…we talked."

"Very well, I guess that I will visit."

"In this envelope is the address; take a cab when you get to Euston Station. It's about fifteen minutes away. A receptionist will tell you the drill when you arrive. Any questions?"

"No, I don't think so…I'm a bit taken aback."

"That's alright. My colleagues in London will look forward to seeing you the day after tomorrow. About 11 A.M. will be about right, if the train runs on time. Oh, and by the way, Mr. Wells said that you would be paid for your day in London, and any incidental expenses, so you shouldn't worry about that."

"Well, goodbye then; nice meeting you, Mr.…I never did get your name; I didn't quite take in your name from your identification card."

"Just call me William."

"Well, thank you Bill."

"No, I'm William, not Bill."

"Oh, I'm sorry…William.

Jesse's lunch with Roland took on a new dimension. William was the talking point. Roland knew no more than she did. He'd been around the factory asking a lot of questions with several key people. He'd evidently spent an hour with Frederick Wells behind closed doors. Roland had no idea what they discussed. He didn't ask, and his father was not telling.

Euston Station, two days later, was cold and damp, and Jesse was glad to be huddled in the cab to an address near to the BBC main building. The receptionist in the Georgian town house was most polite, a demure young lady who Jesse noted most likely had never washed a dish in her life, or boiled an egg, and probably would have been a debutant if the war had not derailed her social life. However, she was very precise. Jesse was to wait in the waiting room for just a few minutes.

A middle-aged woman appeared, tweeds, and a very nice pearl necklace, educated, and looked Jesse straight in the eyes when she shook hands. "Barbara's my name. Look, this is just a meeting place. Let's go."

Barbara waved to the receptionist.

She hailed a cab and very quietly leaned inside the driver's compartment and muttered the address. Jesse was intrigued.

Jesse did not know London well. She tried to remember the street names but they seemed to detour down mews and other side streets, though she did recognize Sloane Square.

The cab stopped outside an impressive looking eighteenth-century house, about five stories high and well maintained given the bombing.

Barbara had made small talk on the way to the new address.

Inside, there was clear and evident security. A uniformed military guard checked Barbara's ID, and Jesse had to sign a register. A lift took them to the third floor. There was a sign on a door along the second corridor they went down, marked in large letters on an impressive plate, PERSONNEL.

From the time that Jesse Birkett walked through that door her life changed; it was never the same again, and she would never quite be the same person, always the lovely and very delightful Jesse, but she would acquire new attributes and skills.

After a series of interviews, the good Barbara ushered her up to the top floor.

There was an impressive set of receptionists, 'gate keepers,' as Roland would term such people, the guardians of very important people behind closed doors.

"Well, Miss Birkett, I'm glad you've agreed to join us."

"I'm still not sure, sir, who the 'us' are?"

"Well, that's just fine. I quite understand."

He was an older man, older than Barbara, maybe mid to late fifties, a fine upright military bearing, a definite twinkle in his eye, and well dressed. He had an educated air, almost lawyer-like, mixed with a military firmness, but he was no Colonel Blimp.

"Let me be the first to welcome you," he paused, " to the Special Operations Executive, SOE for short, much easier to say."

"SOE?"

"Yes, SOE. The prime minister set us up to 'set Europe ablaze,' and we're doing just that."

"How do I fit in?"

"Great question...your languages, French and German. You're very secure and trustworthy; you have courage, young lady, and did a great job during the blitz on Coventry."

"More documentation work?"

"Not quite, Jesse, a little more challenging, wouldn't you say, Barbara?"

"Most definitely, Sir Richard."

Sir Richard, thought Jesse to herself. *This is definitely different.*

Jesse spent an hour with Sir Richard, and was then ushered into another fifth floor office where a special security officer indoctrinated her into the whys and wherefores of the Official Secrets Act, and what he called 'Special Programs.' She signed four separate documents that Barbara and the security officer witnessed. He then commenced to 'read her' into a special program.

Barbara gave Jesse details of when she would start her training, and where she would also go—a separate location in London—for additional specialized and focused language training as Barbara described it. Her other training would be at a country house in Buckinghamshire and at an RAF station near Oxford.

Jesse was a natural linguist. Her mother's very best friend was French. Jesse had always known her as Auntie Marie; she was that close to her. Jesse's mother had met Marie when they were young women, during one of Jesse's mother's many visits to Northern France. They became lifelong friends. Tragedy was to change Marie's life. Her husband died of tuberculosis, and her only child, a small son, died from diphtheria when he was just eight years old. She felt closer to Annie Birkett than anyone else when her life seemed to implode with these great losses. Jesse's mother invited her to stay with the Birkett family at Keresley, near Coventry, giving her time to mourn and gain strength. As the weeks turned into months, it became clear that the two women were inseparable. She treated Annie's three children as her two nephews and niece. "Auntie Marie" came natural to all three children. Jesse was Marie's favorite.

Jesse accompanied her mother and Auntie Marie on many trips back to France as a child, and later as a teenager and young woman. Marie taught her French, read to her in French, and conversed regularly in French. All three women would chat in French as if all three were native born French madams.

Jesse opted for German at school, since she received the very best French language and literature training from Marie. She intuitively picked up German and after five years of German, was set for her School Certificate examination in German. She excelled in the oral examination with a professor from Birmingham University. She received a 'Distinction' in oral German and a high passing grade.

Jesse, therefore, had command of two languages when she met Roland at a local dance at the Women's Institute in Keresley, where both their mothers were active. Jesse could never have foreseen that through working for Roland's father at Coventry Gear and being trusted with the special documentation work, she would now be asked to do more for King and Country than most active members of the armed forces in wartime.

Jesse underwent physical fitness training three times a day for several months, learned to parachute, and did four jumps over Salisbury Plain from different light aircraft, all in low visibility and the third and fourth jumps in the dark. She was trained in small arms use—revolvers and Sten guns. She became an explosives expert and learned how to assemble and detonate small devices from just a few pounds upwards of twenty pounds of high explosive. She was drilled in unarmed combat, and became adroit at defending herself against armed male assailants. She became expert with the deadly use of the knife, poisons, and sniper rifle. Intensive radio training and the use of special codes followed further security training and indoctrination. The most challenging of all was the counter intelligence and resistance to interrogation training. The latter involved, in one instance, ten days of privation, starvation, and physical and psychological abuse by highly trained interrogators who acted like in all regards the Gestapo and the SS. The worst phase of this training involved the use of hypnotism, coupled with physical torture. She survived this training and in the final field testing phase, was dropped into Northern Scotland in mid-winter to execute a rendezvous with simulated local resistance workers. The training involved a deliberately orchestrated betrayal of which Jesse was unaware, until she found herself looking down the barrel of a Lugar pistol with a German SS officer interrogating her about her operation, training, and all she knew about the SOE.

Jesse did not break, and never once wilted under the pressures of the final training. She flew back to England in an RAF transport for debriefing and then two weeks leave.

Jesse Birkett had now joined the elite ranks as an agent of the SOE. Her language training would now be intensified, while she continued to maintain all her other special skills.

When she arrived home on leave, she had to now continue her deception training, convincing her parents and most of all, Roland, that she was working in a classified mail delivery service in the London area, couriering government mail from one location to another. It was her cover story, and she stuck to it meticulously. It worked. Roland believed her. He never asked her any more questions, and she never told.

"Our Jesse has a very special job in London, making sure that the governmental mail gets through between all the right people; we are so proud of her," Jesse's mother would tell her friends at the Women's Institute and the local Land Army ladies working in the fields to help feed a nation that was living on the bare essentials.

The Special Operations Executive had something very different in mind for Jesse.

Chapter Fourteen
INTO FRANCE

Pawns are important pieces on a chessboard. They may not be the holders of absolute power, but they nonetheless play a critical role—without them, there would be no chess. In late 1943, Jesse became a pawn in a very important chess game. She could not know what the grand chess players had in mind for her, a highly trained pawn in a desperate game to save civilization from the Nazi evil. The masters of this great game were people Jesse would never know, never meet, and would not be privy to the moves that they planned on the board that was Europe. A group of American and British military leaders were planning to invade Europe from within the walls of a building on North Audley Street in London, adjacent to Grosvenor Square.

Buried in another equally sequestered and far more covert location, another group of men and women were planning one of the greatest deceptions of military and world history—how to fool the Nazis, how to enter the mindset of the Wehrmacht leadership, German Intelligences, and most of all the demonic psychology of Hitler himself and his key advisers. The objective was to convince the Germans that the Allies would invade Europe in the Pas de Calais Region of Northern France, one of the shortest crossing areas, and on beaches where amphibious assaults could be executed similar to those in North Africa, Sicily, and Anzio. The leaders and designers of this 'Great Deception' had to ensure that Hitler deployed sufficient forces to this area, so that forces that would otherwise oppose the real landings further to the west in Normandy would be seriously depleted. They had to buy time for a successful first assault on the Normandy beaches, so that bridgeheads could be established, and the Allied Armies establish a firm foothold with continuous resupply guaranteed.

The period before Christmas 1943, was the most cheerful holiday season since September 1939. Americans in London and many bases and towns throughout Britain were now a regular feature of everyday British life. They were "over-paid, oversexed, and over here," as one commentator wryly observed. They were very welcome and were made to feel at home by a nation that endured more suffering than most Americans would ever know, except the men of the US Eighth Air Force and the massive influx of GIs training and waiting for the day when they would set foot on mainland Europe.

Jesse would enjoy none of this. She assiduously learned and mastered the local French dialect of the Pas de Calais of France. She assumed a new identity as a farm girl working on a dairy farm and making cheese. She acquired all the necessary skills on farms near to the covert SOE training center.

"Well, Jesse, I know it's been a long wait. You've been very patient. I know you've been kicking your heels. The good news is that it's your turn now to make a difference," said George, her chief instructor. "We've got something very special for you, and it's the night after tomorrow. We'll spend the rest of today and all tomorrow briefing you on where we're going to drop you in, who'll meet you, and what the objectives are. Do you feel ready?"

"Yes, of course, I've been waiting for months. Where am I going—I assume Northern France after all that I've been studying for the past months. I know every road, river, canal, and railway in the Pas de Calais. I know every town and village, the names of the shops, the mayors, the local priests, and the location of all the German units in that area."

"You've done very well; we're proud of you. I know you're itching to go, but the next day and a half will be more important than anything before. We're going to brief you on the mission, and your initial contact. You'll have a pilot who knows the area very well. It will be a very low level drop, Jesse, very low. He will take you in at sea level below the German radar and at a place where we know they will likely not hear the engine. Most of all, Jesse, we are going to brief you on a most sensitive objective that you must under no circumstances ever divulge, except to the two members of the 'Resistance' that we will brief you on."

Jesse had a restless night after the initial briefing. Her mind would not let go of the details of the drop zone, the contact code words, Plan B if one of several things go wrong, and in the worst case her escape route and extraction plan. Her identity, papers, clothing, and appearance had been worked on for months. She had used nothing but her new name, job, location, French family, friends, and her daily routine for several months. That was the easy part.

Day two of her briefing before her night flight into Northern France the following evening was intense. She was tired from a poor night's sleep. The briefers recognized her weariness and took their time.

Jesse was now part of the 'Great Deception.' She, too, at the end of her final briefing day, firmly believed one thing—the Allies would land in Northern France in the spring or early summer of 1944 in the Pas de Calais area of Northern France. Above all else, she was instructed that under pain of death, she must never divulge this critical secret. Only the two members of the local resistance with whom she would plan support for the invasion, should know, no one else.

"Commit suicide, rather than give way, Jesse."

The cyanide pill was her final solution to the ultimate test if torture became intolerable. The vial was the most cleverly concealed on her person even when stripped, beaten, and submerged in freezing water. It was the last resort.

"Avoid capture, at all cost. You just must not be caught. If you are betrayed, play out the double bluff under interrogation. The SS will try to break you in the ways that the Gestapo will not—play on the key things that make your betrayer look like the traitor if you are caught." These words echoed in Jesse's mind. Who would betray her, who could betray the loyal members of the Resistance, now of all times, when the tide had turned, when the Red Army was digging in and destroying the flower of German youth on the Eastern Front? These questions perplexed Jesse's mind, racing now at a thousand miles an hour as she spent her last night in a warm English bed, knowing that her loved ones were less than a hundred miles north of the training center.

The two key codeword names were provided, together with her new family and the two key points of contact. The Resistance had built by late 1943, several layers of internal security to guard against both betrayal and also the effects of SS and Gestapo interrogation.

"I need a sleeping pill tonight, please. I have to get a good night's sleep. I'm exhausted. I hardly slept a wink last night."

"No problem. The doc will fix you up. You'll be able to have a lie in before we drive you down to the field near the south coast where the aircraft will be waiting for you."

"That's good, thank you," Jesse said to George.

"We'll know by late afternoon if the weather will cooperate. It's forecast to be low cloud with some showers. The key is how low? We don't want the cloud cover to be too low." George frowned a little with these last words as he and Jesse parted company.

As Jesse climbed into the unmarked staff car just after lunch the following day, the weather looked good for the night drop.

"Jesse, you're one of the best that we've put through training. Good luck, and remember, take no chances and keep the mission always in mind. Never do anything that can wait if things don't look good. Remember what I've always stressed—be 100 percent certain before making a move." George paused, looked Jesse squarely in the eyes, and the wistful look vanished from his face, "And, Jesse, remember, if things get bad, never hesitate to kill whoever it may be, French or German, don't leave anyone alive to betray you or others." George stiffened and closed the car door.

Jesse waved to him as the car pulled away.

Neither George nor Jesse knew the real truth, that Jesse was a key pawn in the great game to deceive Hitler. The real secret lay elsewhere, with those who had masterminded the very deception in which Jesse would now play her role, with many others, in executing.

As the car disappeared down the driveway of the SOE training center, George sighed. He silently prayed that they had equipped Jesse with all the skills and ingenuity to be successful. Most of all, George knew that above all else,

Jesse would need one outstanding quality—courage. He breathed out a deep breath, smelled the cold early December air, climbed the steps back into the country house, and felt good that Jesse met the need for courage in spades.

The training director was standing in the hallway.

"How was the farewell?"

"Just fine, just fine…she'll do very well. Jesse Birkett is made of very stern stuff."

"Let me get you a drink, George."

Chapter Fifteen
GIVE ME LUCK ANY DAY

As the Lysander circled the drop zone the experienced RAF pilot kept, just a few hundred feet below the cloud base with enough moonlight striking through the gaps in the clouds to see the field and the other markers that identified, beyond all doubt, Jesse's landing area. Jesse crouched in the open doorway, waiting for the pilot's signal. The light flashed below. He circled one more time, losing more altitude. The pilot pulled back on the power just above stall speed, and gave her the thumbs up to jump.

As Jesse controlled the parachute for its short descent, her mind reflected on one comment that had stuck with her throughout her training—"Give me luck any day."

Her luck held. The rain from the previous two days made for a soft landing in the open field. Within minutes friendly hands helped her to her feet as the harness was released, and her newfound friend pointed to a gate at the edge of the field adjacent to a forest.

"Good evening,"…two magic words that warmed Jesse's cold body. The man handed her a very small flask and she sipped the cognac, a precious luxury.

The code words were exchanged in two sequences. The man who had helped her in the field waved a goodbye, and her new guide said, "Follow me," in his distinct dialect. Jesse responded with perfect Pas de Calais French. He opened what looked like a hunting bag and handed her a Lee Enfield rifle and ammunition, letting her know that she was to have this until they reached their destination and they would use the weapons only if they ran into serious trouble. He explained that they would take a circuitous route to the farmhouse and family where she would stay for the next several months.

On the way he spoke quietly, resting from time to time to explain the modus operandi over the next few days and weeks as she became accustomed to the area, and how he ran things with his fellow Resistance worker, who had just helped her in the field. At one stop, near a stream where they had to wade through about eighteen inches of very cold water, they both had another quick sip of his cognac. Here he explained that they would be her only two points of contact and that she would be met and contacted at the times and ways of his choosing. He explained that this would protect her, the Resistance, and the family where she would live. Only he would make contact. Once she became totally familiar with the area, they would operate only at night. He explained in very tender terms that she was to enjoy Christmas and the New Year, and that once January was over they would work hard together, as a team, to lay plans to execute whatever London had in mind. As he tucked away the small silver flask, he looked at her in the moonlight and said with a broad smile, "We have great things to do and little time. We await your instructions. We will advise what is possible, and what is not. Above all, we must avoid compromise. You understand?"

Jesse listened, not wishing to let Jean feel that she may have another agenda. He told her the route that would take them safely to the farmhouse was designed to avoid the German patrols, and was about three times the distance that the road would take, but it was infinitely safer. Jesse nodded agreement.

At one rest point, Jean began to tell Jesse about the local Gestapo and SS organization and who was who, when a wild boar crossed their path in the woods.

"Don't move, don't move," Jean said softly. "They can be quite dangerous. Just wait. It will go away if we do not frighten it. Those tusks can ruin your day!"

The wild boar disappeared. "I would rather shoot the local SS and Gestapo leaders than that poor creature," Jean whispered.

"Are they suspicious of you or any of the networks?" Jesse asked.

"Oh, yes," Jean nodded. "They are constantly looking for evidence to link myself and others to the Resistance. Fortunately they have not had excuses to take reprisals because we have not yet killed any of the worst of the SS and Gestapo. When the time is ripe...," Jean squeezed his rifle, "that will all change."

Jesse mooted, "And what of the Vichy and collaborators...what of them, are they a serious threat?"

"Always, always, Jesse. You cannot trust anyone outside our immediate network. Never talk to anyone unless Paul or I give you the word. There are several people on the payroll of the SS and Gestapo. We know who several of them are. We know their moves and who they see. They receive favors. Men and women. Do not trust any of the women either. Some of them provide favors to both the SS and Gestapo. Our local mayor plays both ends off against the middle—he runs with the hounds one day, and hunts with the fox the next. Don't trust him or any of his friends."

"I see," said Jesse. "Sounds like you have them wired?"

"Yes, but there are always surprises; people who you would think better of."

"And the family I will stay with?"

"Totally loyal, but, and this is important, we do not let them into anything else other than taking you in and providing cover. They know nothing of our organization, how we operate, and nothing at all about our communications and sabotage. We protect them by them knowing nothing. Work on the farm, be a good cheese maker, sell their cheeses, and enjoy their good cooking, but never ever tell them a thing, understand Jesse?"

"Yes, yes, I certainly do."

"Your papers are perfect, your prior history is all in order, and nothing will expose you unless you make a slip. For them, you are what you appear to be—you came from the south after your parents died to find work at a diary farm, to milk, make cheeses, and survive in these tough economic times. The people in London have done a fine job to make your past life authentic. You know your story, stick to it—it will all tie in if the Gestapo or the SS try to backtrack on your life for some reason. We know about how they…. No, enough of that. I need to keep quiet myself about certain things. You see, that's how we survive…by not telling each other things we do not need to know; if we are taken, then tortured, we cannot reveal things that we do not know."

"I understand, Jean. I will not let you or Paul down, ever."

As they made their way through the woods, Jean asked about Jesse's family.

"They think that I am now working in the British Embassy in Bern, Switzerland, translating and couriering documents between embassies in good old neutral Switzerland. I told by mother and father and boyfriend that I could be away for two years."

"I see," said Jean, "that is tough for you. I promise you, we will make you welcome here, but we have God's work to do, we have to rid France of the Nazis, and we are ready for the invasion when it comes."

This was the first time Jean had hinted at his deeply rooted Catholicism and his faith. Jesse was an Anglican, a Protestant, and was well trained to not let religion get in the way of her mission.

"God bless you, Jean, and all free Frenchmen. Your Allied friends cannot wait for the day of reckoning."

"In a few days, Jesse, once you have settled in, we will slowly and surely show you how we track the various German units. London will want your reports in due course. I will show you how and when we communicate, and how they communicate with us."

Jesse inwardly digested all the details that Jean then imparted about the work ahead once the Christmas season passed. She thought to herself that she and she alone must guard against the revelation of the assault on Europe through the Pas de Calais.

As they neared the farm, Jean gently pulled her arm, "Wait a moment, Jesse, I will go ahead, and ensure all is well. Remember, this is the last time I will ever call you by your given name. You are now Marie, and will always be Marie. Only I know your given name. Paul does not know it. You are now Marie. We will only ever use your codename when you communicate, and until such time as London changes it. They may change it very soon."

"I see," said Marie. "When will we know?"

"Normally, at the time of their first transmission to me for you and then, only you will know. I will not need to know."

"But you and I are joined together, Jean, we know what we know about each other."

"Yes," said Jean, "that is the weak link in the whole chain—two of us must know, we must never betray each other if we are captured. Otherwise, we may all go down. A chain is only as strong as its weakest link."

Jesse, aka Marie, looked at Jean as they both prepared to split, with Jean approaching the farmhouse first to ensure that all was well, while Jesse held back in the undergrowth. He looked older than his years, a man in his forties who by the worn look of his face, the stress in his eyes, and the straggly graying hair that hung like straw from underneath his black beret could have been fifteen years older. Jean's physical agility, quick reactions, and piercing glances provided an opposite picture, of a man that was not just fit and healthy, but ready to spring like a coiled tiger once he had found his prey. Jesse felt very comfortable with Jean. During the trek across the wooded countryside, they had quickly built camaraderie and mutual confidence. In Marie, Jean could see the steely temperament and quick mind that would stand them both in good stead in the coming months.

The light in the farm house blinked. Jean returned, bade Marie farewell from the cover of the copse, and said in a low voice that he would soon be back in touch.

Marie entered the farmhouse, and into a new world and a new life.

Her luck had held. She was safe on French soil. A few miles away were the units of the SS and the Wehrmacht Panzer Division Headquarters that commanded the critical Panzer Divisions whose composition, location, and movements were high on her intelligence gathering list. The location and nature of German armor was the single most worrisome element of the Allied planners back in England. As General Eisenhower and the staff of the Allied Expeditionary Force moved location to Southwick Hall in Hampshire, Jesse Birkett could think of nothing but her final briefing before she emplaned for France.

Her short welcome in the middle of the night accomplished, Jesse settled into a cozy bed in a dormer bedroom above the main barn, entered by a side stairwell. She would wash from a stone sink in cold water provided by a stirrup pump on the side of the barn, underneath a slanted wooden roof that provided some protection from the elements. For the rare hot bath and clothes washing she would use the farmhouse. She would eat with the family—man and wife and three children whose ages ran from eight through fourteen— and she would start work in the morning when the cows were herded for the early morning milking. Milk delivery would begin at dawn.

Jesse instantly recognized the tremendous value presented by the farmer's single milk delivery truck, an ancient Citroen that had been nurtured from the 1920s into the 1940s with loving care. From within, and during delivery rounds, Jesse could observe all that transpired on the nearby roads, with passing German convoys, and the various holding areas for the main battle tank of the Wehrmacht, the Tiger Tank. Jesse's command of German would now pay dividends. She had to remember one thing, to never utter a word of German.

Chapter Sixteen
FEBRUARY-MARCH 1944
PAS DE CALAIS, FRANCE

As the winter weather moved from bitter cold, with north easterlies blowing from the North Sea across the coast of the Pas de Calais, to temperatures above freezing, the thoughts of all turned to spring and new beginnings. For Marie there was only one thought, and it was not the weather. The weather during the harshness of January and February had provided ideal cover for her movements and observations of German troop movements. With Jean as her coach, she had mastered the communications procedures with the British built radios provided by SOE.

Marie's codename had been changed several times. She had memorized the sequence of messages that would alert to a coming code name change, a vital security procedure. If Marie did not respond correctly she would not receive further communications from England. Marie never faltered. She was in touch with her SOE handlers, changing communications locations each time with the key objective of avoiding transmission detection by the Gestapo direction finding vans, looking constantly for frequencies outside the German communications bands and frequencies. Jean explained that one of their critical counter- intelligence goals was to know the whereabouts of these vans. He explained that one of their technical people knew when and how to best mask their signals based on local terrain and atmospherics, and reduce what in effect was the omni-directionality of their transmissions. The vans would regularly patrol at night on the assumption that the Resistance would transmit at night. In fact the weather, terrain location, and counterintelligence information on the patrol routes of the direction finding vans drove the times of Marie's transmissions. Similarly, Jean and Marie would give SOE prior notice when they were in a good position and time to receive. On occasions, depending on information to be sent and received, Jean and Marie would be alone once the transmitter had been set up and reception verified. This was sound security procedure based on need to know. Often Jean and Marie would send similar messages on the same themes—German unit insignias, formation numbers, types of equipment with the key command and control locations, and facilities, such as German communications antenna, and most of all the command structure based on Marie's intimate knowledge of Wehrmacht, SS, and Gestapo organizational structure. From this information, SOE could soundly estimate force structure and dispositions. All their information was encoded; a laborious and time consuming task when using Morse code. Marie and Jean had different codes for each of the German units, strengthening security, but requiring both of them to be sure that their memories were good. When Marie finished training, she could recite the codes in her sleep, as if she was saying her twelve times tables.

As February ended and the weather turned spring-like for a few days and the cloud cover diminished, Jean reported to Marie that his people had sighted more RAF air reconnaissance flights, some at quite low level, with the Germans responding with anti-aircraft fire. None of the specially equipped Spitfires had been hit from all the reports received. Incoming messages from SOE intensified requests for data on the location and numbers of the Wehrmacht and SS Panzer divisions and their apparent command structure.

Marie had made two critical breakthroughs in penetrating German units. Senior Nazi officers liked their food and wine, living high on the hog with good French wines, cognacs, and champagne for the general officers, and amongst their food demands, local cheeses. Marie had unobtrusively started to supply the officers' messes at four locations with cheeses, all French country houses sequestered by the Nazis, and employing local people as cooks, maids, cleaners, and valets for the senior officers. Marie assumed, and rightly so, that Jean had a good handle on all this, and that he was tapping every source for information.

Marie's collection at these locations turned to gold. She overheard critical conversations between high ranking officers that none of the local French people could understand, including Jean and his fellow Resistance leaders. She was the only fluent German speaker in the area amongst the Resistance and, furthermore, Marie had detailed working knowledge from her training of the whole German command and control structure as best understood by British military intelligence. Familiarity with German officers increased. She knew their individual cheese preferences, and had direct access to the kitchens and dining areas. She would supply freshly baked bread, and butter from the dairy. The downside became evident to Marie. Several of the officers took a shine to her, and the ages ranged from the young majors and colonels to the general officers. Several patted her bottom as a matter of routine, and two tried to fondle her in the kitchens. Her savior was their poor command of French. She blew them off with friendly gestures so as not to aggravate them. However, at the SS Headquarters one of the more senior majors not only took a particular fancy to Marie, but he saw her as a possible source, an informer.

Marie was on her guard from the moment SS Major Carl Gustav Fritzmeyer made his first advances in what was very passable Parisian French. Marie saw also the advantages. He was a source. She could feed him disinformation in very minor, ostensibly innocent ways, particularly with anything relating to local

Resistance organizations. At the same time, she could simply listen, particularly when he was talking in German with his brother officers and junior staff. Marie played the game, as innocently as appearances would allow. She was also cognizant that as a newcomer to the area the locals would notice any fraternizing with the Germans, a potential downside.

By early March 1944, Marie was seeing the major two, sometimes three times a week, in the evenings in the local *auberges* and taverns. He paid for dinner and drinks. His insidious questioning was clear to Marie, but she with incredible deftness played the SS officer like a fiddle, with him totally unaware of her clever maneuvering and discreet answers to his many questions. Her command of French permitted the most subtle manipulation of several tense periods of questioning by him, with him always assuming that she was an innocent uneducated farm girl.

The dynamics changed.

SS rules forbade sexual encounters with locals for fear of compromise, but for SS Major Carl Fritzmeyer, Marie presented a target of opportunity for sexual gratification. Marie was on her guard, recognizing the signs and symptoms of a man that was out of control. At the same time, he presented an information target. Could she keep him at bay while gleaning as much information from him as possible? Jean's advice was simple—get as much from him as possible, but do not have sex with him under any circumstances. Information indicated that he had already been treated for venereal disease, and was most likely still infected. Local doctors had been brought in to treat several German officers who had been cohabiting with prostitutes in the port areas. He was one of them.

Marie thought of Roland, and made a personal inner commitment to never let one of these Nazis force their attention on her. She comforted herself by recalling several of Frederick Wells' best expletives about Hitler and his cohorts. She would smile to herself, picturing him denouncing the master race in his own inimitable way. She felt secure.

The SS major had other ideas.

"You are very beautiful, Fraulein Marie," he would exhort, "quite the best of a very poor bunch of local whores and peasants. You are well endowed, my dear, I think we could do well together. I can make sure you have some benefits. I can take care of you, and make sure you and your family eat well."

"I don't understand," Marie played dumb.

"Oh, I can provide you with nice things, maybe even a trip to Paris when I have my next leave, unless of course, that bastard Churchill and his stooge Eisenhower try to rock our boat."

"You will have to explain, I don't understand."

"Very simple, you let me have what I want and I will take care of you. Maybe you can also keep an eye out for me, you know?"

"What do you want me to do?"

"Very simple, you just tell me a little on what you see going on around here, people who are out at night after the curfew, any strange happenings, anyone with a gun or going to meetings at night, that sort of thing. Do you understand?"

"Yes, I think I do. I want to help you."

"Good, good, my dear, that's wonderful, we say *wunderbar* in German. Perhaps, if I can get a staff car for the night, we can go to one of the towns to the south for the night, you know, out of sight of the locals?"

"But I have to work. I have to be up by four, milk the cows, and then do chores in the dairy. I have no time. I have to make the cheeses."

"We'll figure it out, my dear. Don't you worry? Maybe next week, when I have a night free, we can spend the night together."

Marie sighed as if neither affirmation nor denial. She needed time to plan.

He kissed her, and then fondled Marie in a crude and direct manner, grabbing her breasts like an animal. He then backed off, and departed with a pathetic wave, leaving Marie somewhat stultified, wanting to kill him there and then. Her two concealed small stiletto knives were her last means of defense—one on each side of her upper thighs, concealed inside a waistband. She inwardly told herself to keep under control, and play out this game of cat and mouse for all it was worth.

The next radio message to England was short and simple. A reliable SS source indicated that the SS Panzer divisions would be staying in the area for the time being. Wehrmacht headquarters' staff had been augmented—several additional SS and Gestapo staff had joined from Berlin. The SS and Gestapo were intensifying local surveillance, with many more roadblocks, ID checks in the towns and villages, and additional DF vans were patrolling round the clock. No one was allowed access to the coastline and Nazi fortification areas along the main beaches where the Nazis clearly expected Allied landings. Citizens were randomly seized and interrogated.

The last day of March 1944, saw Marie about to face her sternest test.

Chapter Seventeen
KEEP THE HOME FIRES BURNING

Across the English Channel, Britain was now safe from any air raids. The balance of air power had shifted decisively to RAF Bomber Command and the United States Eighth Air Force. The Allies were beginning massive raids on German industrial centers. German cities were not spared. Air Chief Marshal Sir Arthur Harris at Bomber Command Headquarters was unrelenting in executing strategic bombing. The RAF and the US Eighth Air Force were sending thousand bomber raids over Nazi Germany.

Meanwhile, a different kind of war was being executed by two separate groups that would define the genius of British intelligence for the rest of time. One was at Bletchley Park and the other was divided between multiple locations in London and country houses. In short, the masterminds of reading German communications and deceiving the Nazi mindset was in top gear. To the north of much of this activity, in the English Midlands, Frederick and Roland Wells continued to work round the clock and play their crucial roles to keep the RAF supplied. Coventry was now no longer subject to aerial destruction. The Luftwaffe had been brought to heel.

Roland made one of his regular calls to Don Finlay in his new position as Eleven Group Fighter Command's group engineering officer.

"Don, how's the job going?"

"I miss flying, Roland. Promotion has grounded me. I like the job, but it's not quite the same as when I was in 54 Squadron at the height of the Battle of Britain, and then when they gave me command of 41 Squadron. When I was promoted in August '41, I was really pleased with myself, as you know—remember the party we all had? But I miss the front end. I miss the action, Roland."

"I can feel it in your voice. But you must be pretty busy?"

"Well we are, getting ready to provide the group with all the engineering support needed for when the invasion takes place. We are going to have to keep air to ground support going 'round the clock."

"Air to ground support?"

"Yes, that's the new buzz phrase—fighter command will not have much of the Luftwaffe left to fight in the air, but we will need to support the Army by attacking tanks, artillery, railways, bridges, artillery, and the like."

"I see a whole new era of air power."

"You've got it. But now to a little good news, and we know each other well enough to tell you that I am keeping my fingers crossed that this happens."

"You're going back to flying."

"Sort of, or at least if I have my way and finagle things the right way I will get myself in the cockpit by hook or by crook, Roland."

"So, what's up?"

"Possible command of 608 Squadron in the Middle East, flying Hudsons— not quite the Spitfire, but it'll do—better than being grounded doing a staff job while the war is still in its final stages."

"That sound great, Don, you deserve it. When you got your DFC in '42, it was clear that they couldn't keep you on the ground. Hell, what a waste of talent. I gather that your fine leader Park is on his way up, thank God. My dad follows who is who in the RAF. He likes Tedder a lot."

"Yes, he's right. Keith Park survived the purge when Dowding was put out to pasture. He's done a brilliant job as the AOC in Malta, keeping the Hun pinned down in the Mediterranean, denying the Axis powers supply to North Africa. The buzz is that he's on his way up to four stars and command of the RAF in the Far East, supporting the Thirteenth Army in nailing the Japs. If you ask me, and anyone in the RAF who knows anything about command, Park should be running the air show for the invasion of Europe. Portal will never do it. Portal sees Leigh-Mallory and that whole crowd of senior RAF staff who moved upwards with Leigh-Mallory as his boys, the "in crowd." Park is not and never will be one of them."

"Why doesn't Tedder push for Park?"

"He's got to keep on good relations with the chief of the air staff and I reckon that once Churchill decides that Portal is at the end of his career, he will make Tedder the boss, wait and see; I will bet money on it. Plus, the fact Tedder wants to run the Allied air show, that's his goal in life; pushing Park will not help him."

"I see…all politics. Thank God for people like you, Don, the guys who really do the fighting."

"You're very kind. Enough of me, what about you? How's that great dad of yours and have you heard from Jesse? Is she still overseas?"

"Well, my dad is working as hard as ever. Mother wants him to take some time off now that the tide's turned in the war, but he won't relent. The most he'll do is a weekend in London, and then he sees all his Ministry of Aircraft Production buddies. I have not heard from Jesse since she left. She's in Berne, Switzerland, and they keep her on a tight leash—no communications. Evidently a lot of sensitive communications move around in good old neutral

Switzerland, and she is their chief in country courier. She's not allowed calls or anything. We got a call from a man down in London in the Foreign Office, passing on a message from her that she was fine, missed us all, and sent us all big hugs and kisses."

"Well, at least she's in a safe spot, and Switzerland must have plenty of good food and wine. She'll be fine. When this is all over you'll have to make an honest woman of her, Roland?"

"Now then, Don…you and my mother!"

"Change of subject, have you heard from any of the famous four, or our other Jesse in the States?"

"I got a letter from Jesse Owens about three weeks ago, but have not heard a thing from Godfrey and the boys," said Roland.

"Well, Godfrey is fighting with the Royal Artillery and I know that Freddie Wolff is fighting with the Oxfordshire and Buckinghamshire Light Infantry. I would bet my next paycheck that they are getting ready for the invasion," said Don.

"How's Jesse doing?"

"This is just reading between the lines—on the surface he seems to be doing fine, but I sense that he is still really upset by the lack of recognition. In two letters to me he's repeated one incident in particular that clearly grates with him, and I don't blame him at all. I can understand why."

"What's that about?" asked Don.

"Well, he's keeping himself and his family going pretty well, but it's clear he faces a lot of prejudice. In two long letters he's dwelt a lot on what happened when he got home in '36. Big parade in New York City, one of those ticker-tape parades that the 'Yanks' do so well, just a great event and he's there as the hero of the hour, and guess what? At the end of the parade, they have a big reception for him at the, oh what is the name of that big fancy hotel in New York?"

"The Waldorf Astoria?"

"Yes, that's it. He's told to take the freight elevator. He's not allowed to mix with all the fine white folk and go up with them to some huge fancy ballroom where he's being honored. Can you believe that? I can't, but it's true. Their greatest athlete of all time, and they treat him like dirt. When the war's over, I'm going to ask dad to pay for him to come over here, and get him to do a tour—talk about athletics and his experiences in 1932 and 1936, and encourage our athletes."

"Great idea, if he'll come. I sense, Roland, Jesse wants to be truly honored in his own country. That's my take. He loves the Brits, but what he wants and needs, is the satisfaction of being truly accepted as an all-American athlete, irrespective of his color."

"Don, I've got to go, my dad wants us all in a meeting on the hour."

"I've got to rush too—figuring out engineering support once we put fighter squadrons back in mainland Europe."

"I envy you. I'll trade with you."

"Roland, never say that, you do great and important things. Without you and the thousands with you, we would not have had aircraft to fly. My Merlins have never let me or my men down once. Now hear that. Let's talk soon. If I hear more about the new posting, you'll be the first to know. Out here."

"Out here, too, Don; take care."

As Wells and Finlay ended their conversation, another important meeting was taking place between the leaders of the Twenty Committee, people from Bletchley Park, MI5, MI6, and the SOE. One of the several key people that would be affected by this special gathering was the young lady about whom Roland and Don had just conversed—the *courier par excellence* in Berne, Switzerland.

Twenty stood for XX, the Roman numerals for the number twenty, and also 'double cross.' But, who was double crossing who? The answer was one of the best kept secrets of World War II, together with the existence of Bletchley Park the Enigma secret and the Ultra product from Enigma. The Twenty Committee controlled German agents captured in Britain, and then used their identities and communications procedures to deceive the Nazis and their intelligence echelons in the Abwehr, the SD, the SS, and the Gestapo. It was a masterful plan executed with consummate skill and cunning. The leader of the Twenty Committee was John Cecil Masterman.

"Call to order, please gentlemen," said J. C. Masterman, as the collective great minds of the five key British intelligence and special operations organizations talked amongst themselves before their meeting began.

"We have one critical objective at this morning's meeting and one alone— we have to submit to the prime minister and to the supreme allied commander, General Eisenhower, our final plans for ensuring that our deception of the Nazis about the location of the D-Day landings is totally assured. The P. M. has made it clear—we cannot and must not fail in this regard. No medals for getting this wrong. I think that we all understand."

"We are all clear on this, John, but may we ask up front, please, what are the guidelines—how far can we go in the final analysis? We have several key agents on the ground in Northern France. They are all at risk," said Harry Hinsley from Bletchley Park.

"I'm with you Harry, but the prime minister, the chiefs of staff, and Eisenhower have made it clear—nothing, absolutely nothing, should be in our way to continue the deception right up to the moment of the landings, otherwise our people could be butchered on the beaches in the thousands; it could be the worst military disaster in history."

"Got it, John, we all needed clarification," commented Hinsley.

"Now, to our most sensitive agent," Masterman paused. "Are all the doors and windows closed and guarded?"

"Yes, we're fine, sir," said the joint committee secretary and record keeper from MI6.

"Well, the P. M. and we ourselves are the guardians of whom we speak; even Eisenhower does not know this, the P. M. has never wanted to risk any possible leak of Admiral Canaris' key role as one of our best agents and intelligence suppliers."

In one sentence, Masterman reminded the group of the fact that Admiral

William Canaris, the head of the German Abwehr, was a British spy—a man who hated Hitler and the destruction of his beloved Germany by the Nazis—and that this was the most sensitive of all British secrets, together with Enigma and the Ultra intelligence product.

"Now, to some bad news. We are still checking through MI6 sources, but the evidence is that Admiral Canaris has been placed under arrest."

There was total silence in the room, as Masterman paused. The tension was so strong it could have been cut with a knife.

"How do we know, Bletchley's seen nothing in the traffic."

"That's why," said Masterman, "he's gone silent."

"Oh, my God," said the secretary to the inner War Cabinet who knew all.

"Yes, he has not communicated for over three weeks. He had indicated in his very last communication through MI6's link with him in Spain that Heinrich Himmler suspected him and that the SS were watching him night and day and reading all his communications."

"Did our elimination of Reinhard Heydrich in Prague have anything to do with this? Did they suspect that the head of the Abwehr was tied to MI6 via our European links?"

"We don't know, is the simple answer," said Masterman in a low gravelly voice. "We just don't know. What we do know is that that the SS and the SD are now in charge. The Abwehr is clearly being reorganized, downgraded, we know that, and this is why we think that Wilhelm Canaris, the bravest of the bravest Nazi haters, is gone."

"I see," said Hinsley, "that accounts for why we are seeing all the SS and SD traffic in Northern France, and very little or any Abwehr communications. We put it down to increased security—we assessed that the Abwehr were using more couriers from Berlin…clearly not."

Masterman ordered that the Bletchley team concentrate all efforts on Himmler's SS communications to support the Double Cross operation.

The inter agency committee then spent three hours between 0900 and 1200 working out and agreeing on the detailed master plan for deception and intelligence operations in support of the deception plan for April and May.

Toward the end the meeting, the two lead Bletchley Park officers made very pointed comments.

"Have we assessed the impact of our communications plans and how and what SOE will communicate to our agents in the Pas de Calais area? It could be very dangerous for all of them if the SS and Gestapo react in the ways that we want. They will intensify their searches and direction finding."

"Several of our key agents will be in great danger," said the most senior SOE officer present. "Giving away our codes deliberately, however devious and subtle we plan to conceal them as a double bluff, the fact remains that we increase the risk to our agents on the ground and the whole Resistance organization that supports them."

"I understand," said Masterman, "but we have our orders and this is one of the most effective ways for us to convince the Wehrmacht leadership that we are landing in the Pas de Calais, and not Normandy. Once they know that our agents are apparently under strict orders to support the invasion in the Pas de Calais, they will be convinced that this is where we will land."

Several people sighed, but no one challenged the comment. This was policy, irrevocable policy, from the very top, from Churchill.

The head of the SOE was fearful. He knew that the overall detailed plan was not only brilliant in conception and would work; however, it was nonetheless designed in ways that would, by default, place all the British SOE agents in the Pas de Calais area at increased risk.

As he closed his staff car door and drove down the long driveway, with the spring flowers beginning to bloom and the leaves emerging, the SOE leader thought of Admiral William Canaris being tortured by the SS, and then his mind turned to SOE's critical intelligence suppliers and saboteurs in Northern France. He could see all their faces, and they were all women.

Jesse Birkett's face would not leave his mind. She was in the middle of deadly action.

Chapter Eighteen
THE PAS DE CALAIS, FRANCE
APRIL 1-JUNE 5, 1944

The German signal posts and all their wires splintered and crashed to the ground as the explosive charges did their work. Jean, Paul, and their small teams of saboteurs hit multiple Wehrmacht communication sites at the same moment, timed to take down as much of the land line communications in their area as possible. Along with the military communications, the Resistance also hit the Vichy French telephone networks, including several sub stations, and the main telephone exchange in the area. Several French civilians were badly injured in the attacks.

That same night, several known collaborators simply disappeared, never to be seen again. They were removed from their homes, eliminated, and then buried in several locations in the woods surrounding the area. The price of collaboration, of betrayal, and of heinous treachery was paid in full. Those collaborators remaining now lived in terror. Any further collaboration and they, too, would be gone. Part of the SOE plan was to leave enough collaborators to feed disinformation to the Nazis.

In one memorable meeting with a senior Vichy official, a collaborator par excellence, Jean, made it very clear, "My friend, if you so much as breathe a word about the Allied landings in the area, I will personally gut you, like a fish from the river, and hang your entrails on the bridge. Do you understand?" Jean knew that he would be betrayed, the information passed on, and so he and Paul and the other key Resistance leaders executed Plan B, their exit strategy into the surrounding woods and countryside—new beards, different clothes, new papers, and a whole set of new procedures to avoid capture and torture.

Now was the time London had instructed to set the area ablaze, and use all the explosives and weapons that they had assiduously stored after each SOE drop. The caches were spread well out, and now with great relish and enthusiasm, Jean and his men and women began systematic sabotage and assassinations of Nazis caught on the roads at night. In their searches of the wooded areas, several German patrols were lured into ambushes by scents deliberately left to fool the hounds used by the SS and Gestapo. No one was spared. Bodies were buried on the spot…the hounds shot.

The SS and Gestapo requested Berlin to send additional intelligence support and more troops.

Marie's SS protégé was given unequivocal orders by his SS Obersturmbannführer, "Find these people now, use whatever it takes to get information, and then kill them. If they resist capture, take no prisoners. We will send a message to the people here. We mean serious business."

"And reprisals?" said major Fritzmeyer. "You mentioned reprisals earlier."

"Round up ten men from each of the villages near to where our men have been killed by the Resistance, take them into the woods, and shoot them."

"Is that an order, Herr Obersturmbannführer?"

"You hear me, Major, that's an order from Herr Himmler himself. Now, go execute. Report to me when you have completed these orders. As far as the Resistance is concerned, take no prisoners, is that clear?"

"Yes, Herr Obersturmbannführer. Heil Hitler!"

"Heil Hitler. You're a good man, Fritzmeyer. Do a good job and I will recommend you for promotion. The Allies will land in this area; that is for sure. I will need all the good men that I have. Now go, get to these tasks."

Fritzmeyer departed the SS Headquarters building and went back to his unit to plan and execute his evil tasks. Also in his warped and vicious mind was how he would seduce the young French woman, extract information from her, and have his way with her. If she would not cooperate his plan was simple—he would torture her, and then, well, the SS major thought, *she is disposable like this entire French rabble—peasants not worthy of the Herrenvolk, the master race, the Aryans destined to rule the world.*

Marie was milking the cows late afternoon when Fritzmeyer appeared in the milking shed, two days after the atrocities had been committed in the area. Her farm and the family had remained unscathed by the local killings. She and the Resistance knew who had perpetrated these evil deeds. Fritzmeyer and his SS troops had the blood of innocent French civilians on their hands.

After a series of curt comments and questions about her availability, Fritzmeyer ordered in a high pitched voice, "Meet me tonight. I want to talk more with you. You and I need to have a little chat. Think about it. You better be cooperative, young woman. I need information. You can help."

"Yes, Herr Fritzmeyer," Marie uttered quietly. "Whatever you say, I will help all I can."

"Good, good, that's what I like to hear. I will pick you up at seven o'clock. Wear one of those pretty farm dresses. No, on second thought, wear that dress I bought for you in Berlin. I like that dress. It shows off your body well."

Marie loathed his sneering voice, Hoch Deutsch accent, and inwardly hated him for what he and his men had done over the previous two days. This was now war. The Resistance would fight to the end, whatever the cost.

As Fritzmeyer closed the door to his SS staff car behind Marie later that evening, the SS major had several agendas.

They chatted as they drive down the country lanes. The May flowers were out and the woods were garlanded in resplendent spring flowers. Marie loved the spring.

Fritzmeyer stopped the car, and said that he wanted to walk down to the river and talk. She had no choice.

At the river bank, foliage hid their whereabouts and the sun was fading. He insisted that they sit on the ground adjacent to some bushes. He began his not so subtle interrogation.

The questions flowed, one after the other—who did she know who might work in the Resistance, who was out at night, what were the local rumors, who was bragging about killing Germans, who did not appear for work, who was hiding British agents, and so it went on, an endless spate of questions. Marie deftly answered all his questions, weaving lies within lies, deception within deception. When he fired one of his leading questions, she was ready, "Well, young Marie, tell me, when are the locals expecting an invasion?"

"Soon, I think, later this month."

"How do you know?"

"I heard some people chatting in the Post Office. Some men were saying that the Allies would be here soon, here in the Pas de Calais."

"Who are these men? Tell me who they are."

"They were men I have not seen before…strangers. I will tell you next time I see them. One of them had a scar on his cheek, a big scar, quite unmistakable. He was quite old, maybe in his fifties, and had a strange accent, not from here."

"How many?"

"Three…there were three. I will recognize them again if I see them; I will tell you, I promise."

As he uttered approval, the SS major started to fondle Marie. He placed his right hand on her thigh, and then started to run his hand up her leg to her crotch. He kissed her in a forceful manner, moving his right hand to her breasts, pulling back her dress and exposing them.

Fritzmeyer then went further than he had earlier in physical encounters with Marie. He forced himself on top on her and ran his right hand up her dress. He then pulled at her dress, the dress that he had bought in Berlin.

Marie now knew one thing. Fritzmeyer was going to rape her.

He undid his trousers and pulled off his boots in an ungainly fashion, and tugged at his trousers so as to expose himself. He was hot, saliva running down his chin, and he had a glare that gave Marie all the courage she now needed. These were the eyes of, not just a rapist in action; this was the look of a demented, evil, and cruel murderer.

Marie relaxed, as if to encourage him, and hoped that he would lessen his grip on her. He did just that, thinking Marie was succumbing. She uttered the most hypocritical words of her life, "You look so magnificent; what a fine German soldier you are, and you're all mine."

"Thank you, my dear," Fritzmeyer sneered.

These were the last words that he would speak.

As he fiddled with his penis, striving like an animal to insert himself into Marie, she suddenly, with great stealth and skill, drove the blade of her concealed stiletto into Fritzmeyer's left side…hooking the knife into his heart, and bringing her right knee with great force into his genitals. He gasped, his eyes bulged, blood appeared from his mouth, and Marie forced the blade deep inside his heart, turning the knife.

In her best German, Marie said to Fritzmeyer in unmistakable tones, "You Nazi bastard, this is for what you did to all those innocent people. Now die, you evil pig." As she used the word *schweinhund,* Fritzmeyer convulsed, realizing with his dying breaths that Marie was with the Resistance. He stared at her, stultified. The air expelled from his lungs, she rolled him off her, and quickly dressed herself.

Within minutes, Marie gathered heavy rocks from the side of the river, opened his tunic, and filled it with stones. She did the same inside his trousers. She closed his trousers and tunic, the heavy weight of the rocks bulging from his body. She took his pistol and ammunition pouch, money, and identity cards. She stripped him of all his possessions.

Marie dragged him to the side of the river, and let his body slide into the water. She pushed him out, and she watched his body sink without trace.

The SS staff car started at first firing. Marie breathed relief. She drove it down the road for a mile or so, praying that no Nazi patrol appeared. She headed off into the woods, down a track that she knew well for about three miles, and then ploughed off the track into an area that had light gorse without major trees to obstruct her. The vehicle would not be found here, at least not for a long time.

After collecting enough gorse to feed a long taper leading many feet from where she stood to start the inferno, Marie lit the gorse and the trail that led along the ground and then up into the gasoline tank ignited perfectly. She quickly turned and ran, diving beneath the protection of a bank covered in spring wild flowers. The car burst into flames as the tank exploded.

As Marie took the most circuitous of routes to the nearest Resistance safe house, she knew several things as the light faded. She could never return to the farmhouse. Once the major's disappearance became known, the SS and the Gestapo would pay her farm a visit. She would be interrogated and tortured. Fritzmeyer bragged about his French girlfriend. They had been seen together by many of his henchmen. She knew that he must have briefed his leaders that she was a target. His final interrogation of her was clearly part of his plan.

Her mind came up with the only viable story that would save her French family and others—she and Fritzmeyer deserted, knowing that the Allies were coming soon—he has run off with her to find love and romance, and surrender to the Allies. This story will be told by her French family and the Resistance will subtly inject this into the local mindset, berating Marie for running off with a Nazi, even though he has deserted.

"Marie, I have good news, and also very bad news," said Jean as he related to her in the Resistance safe house, buried in the woods many miles from the nearest German patrol route.

"What's happened," said Marie fitfully.

"Well, our story has worked so far. Your absence with the SS major's absence seems to have worked. The Nazis are searching for you and him. We put it out that you have both gone to Paris to marry and hide until the Allies arrive."

"But what is bad, Jean?"

"Very bad," said Jean. "They have taken Paul. We can only assume that they have either cracked our codes or we have a traitor in our midst. While you have been in hiding, the Wehrmacht has brought additional Panzers into the whole area. They clearly think an invasion is coming. They are building up their defenses dramatically."

"But, what of the codes? What do you mean?"

"The last two weeks or so while you have been hiding out, the SOE changed the code format. Maybe it was not as clever as before. My gut tells me that the Germans are reading the SOE codes. They are one step ahead of us. We blew the railway lines into Calais the other night. Paul was taken on his way back. I pray that he does not talk. We are all in danger."

"My God," said Marie. "Time maybe for 'Plan Bravo' as my trainer called it."

"What do you mean, Marie, what do you mean?"

"It's time for you and me to leave, Jean, and soon."

"Leave, I cannot leave, I will not leave. When the Allies invade I want to be here. I want to kill those bastards who murdered my people, and kill those Vichy swine who betrayed us all."

"Send a message to London, Jean; do it quickly, please. Just say one short message, 'Newton's apple has fallen.' Do you understand, Jean?"

"Yes, I understand. How long it will take for them to respond I do not know. After Paul was taken, I sent the key abort message. There is no way the Nazis could understand this."

"Good, well done. That is critical. I have lost track of time. Let's open that bottle of wine. I need a good drink. What day is it today?"

As Jean fumbled to open the wine bottle, he uttered the propitious words, Marie, it's June 5. There's a good moon tonight and good weather tomorrow. The weather will clear."

Chapter Nineteen
D-DAY
JUNE 6, 1944

The SS Panzer divisions and Wehrmacht infantry and artillery divisions started to leave the Pas de Calais area and head westward to Normandy late on June 6, once the OKW leadership realized that there would not be a second landing in the Pas de Calais. Normandy was it. The Allies had landed to the west on five beaches, and there would be no second landing front in the Pas de Calais.

The great deception worked, but at a price. In the bowels of the SS headquarters, Paul's torture continued. His body and mind were exhausted. Nothing would make him talk. He had no cyanide pill, no quick way out. They planned to kill him either way, Paul figured.

Over the succeeding days, the Resistance mined the key roads and bridges leading out of the Pas de Calais. They hit the railway lines, the telephone poles, the Nazi fuel dumps, and wherever the terrain provided cover and quick escape, they sniped at units moving down the roads heading west toward Normandy, shooting the highest ranking officers that they could spot through their binoculars.

The SS and Gestapo leadership would not yield. They did not all head west with the main German forces. They figured that, at some point, they had to clear their area of any Resistance movements that would help the advancing Allies coming out of Normandy and heading toward Paris, and then the 'Fatherland.'

Jean gave his orders—they will take no prisoners, spare no one in their searches and sweeps—attack them before they find us. The Resistance in the Pas de Calais unleashed a whirlwind that the SS and Gestapo could not have envisaged.

Over the next forty-eight hours, the Resistance held Vichy and collaborators at gunpoint as they were forced to call their SS and Gestapo handlers to meetings with them, to provide the latest information. The SS and Gestapo ran into well laid traps, ambushed by men and women with the weapons they had waited to use for several years—machine guns, mortars, and the latest British sniper rifles. The traitors were summarily shot once they had served their purposes.

Once the SS realized that the Resistance was now operating at full strength, Paul's time had come. He never faltered, he never gave in, silent to the end, as the SS guards took him into the courtyard of their beleaguered headquarters, and shot him and a group of British Commandos who had been captured after they had landed by glider and destroyed one of the critical bridges across the river, preventing the Panzers from taking the shortest route west. Paul's body was placed in a cart and left in the center of the local village.

As Marie begged Jean to let her be part of the Resistance group that would attack the SS headquarters to avenge Paul, he made one simple comment to her. "Marie, you have done enough. It is time for you to go. We will avenge Paul. You killed Fritzmeyer. That is enough, together with all the great information that you have given London. There can be no change to the plan. You leave tonight. The moon is good, and the weather will permit the landing."

"I want to be with you in the attack on the SS Headquarters!"

"No, Marie, the answer is no. While we give the SS hell, you will fly out of here. The next time we meet will be in better circumstances; trust me, we will meet again. This is not goodbye; it's *au revoir*, until the next time."

Marie embraced Jean.

As the SOE Lysander circled the field, Marie stood with her solitary Resistance companion, a man she had never seen before. They chatted about the night operation going on six miles away. They could hear the chatter of gunfire even at this distance—heavy machine guns and mortars. The night sky was illuminated with shells bursting. Jean and his team were indeed giving the SS hell. Paul was avenged that night and every night until the Germans were driven from France by the advancing Allies.

The Lysander pilot did a pinpoint landing, with the engine revving as Marie climbed quickly into the cabin, pulled the door to, and the pilot lifted off, skimming the trees, and heading toward the coast and England at the lowest possible altitude, darting from side to side to avoid known German gun emplacements and anti-aircraft batteries.

The massive firefight at the SS headquarters took up the attention of the remaining German forces in the area, rushing down roads that were mined and strewn with fallen trees, to be met with a hail of machine gun fire from multiple locations, hidden in the woods alongside the roads. The lead-destroyed vehicles blocked the roads and created chaos. The Resistance snipers went to work, picking off one by one the German soldiers seeking cover alongside the roads, and strafed the Germans with heavy machine guns and mortars.

This was the beginning of the end for the Nazis in occupied France.

As the Lysander approached the English coast, a wave of emotion came over Jesse, aka Marie. The tears came down her face. The pilot had no concept of what his precious passenger had achieved. Her thoughts were only for those she left behind, and for Paul and his family, for Jean, and for her French family. As the Lysander landed at the RAF base she could remember only two words, Jean's last words to her, *au revoir*.

As she stepped out of the Lysander, a friendly hand greeted her.

"Welcome home, Jesse, welcome home; it's so good to see you safe and well."

George hugged Jesse. They walked to the officers' mess and, for Jesse, the war was over.

Chapter Twenty
THE OLYMPIC GAMES
LONDON
1948

Nineteen forty-eight was a memorable year in Britain. Three years from Victory in Europe Day and Victory over Japan Day—VE and VJ days, to use the vernacular. Britain was hosting the first Olympic Games after the end of World War II.

Food and gasoline rationing proliferated. Children had their candy or 'sweets' rationed, using ration books as the children queued to buy their favorite candies—licorice allsorts, dolly mixtures, and the like. Chocolate was still in short supply. Luxuries were only for the rich and famous. As Britain rebuilt itself and occupied Europe with the other Allies, the one bright spot on the horizon was the opening of the 1948 Olympic Games in London. It was a memorable occasion, and a great coming together of nations after years of conflict, death, and destruction. It was a time for peaceful competition and international well being.

The British stadium was a fitting finale to an era when stadiums had been used for purposes other than the pursuit of sport. It symbolized all that was good about the competing nations—their commitment to peace and prosperity, a new hope, and a new beginning.

The Wells family alighted from two cars for the opening ceremony of the Games. Frederick Wells insisted on driving his wife from their hotel in central London to the stadium. The chauffeur was given time off. Wells wanted to drive through the streets of London on this propitious occasion. In the second car were Jesse and Roland Wells, married during the war after Jesse retuned from her time abroad. Their two children were left at home, just a little too young to cope with the occasion. They were staying at the Cumberland Hotel, at Marble Arch, where they had spent their honeymoon nights in a city that was still scarred and recovering from the blitz. For them it was a homecoming, whatever the state of the buildings in London. The world was at peace and their family was together. Jesse stilled missed her older brother, John, killed in HMS Hood, chasing the German battleship Bismarck. He was still deeply in her memory. Fortunately, John was the only person in the Birkett-Wells family to be killed in the war. Wells senior was so very grateful that no one else from both families had perished, having lost his brother Reginald on the Western Front in World War I.

The four family members made their way to their seats.

"How was dinner with Don?" asked Frederick Wells.

"It was marvelous," said Jesse, beating Roland to the response. "He's such a wonderful person. He and Roland reminisced all night, I just listened, and it was magical hearing all their stories. I love to hear about Berlin in 1936."

"It was great, Dad, we had a fine time. I wish the children were old enough to meet him. They're just a bit too young to understand and appreciate what he's achieved."

Frederick Wells paused for a moment, sensing some regret in his son's voice.

"Roland, I think the world of him, too, but you know, Son, I think what you did in the war was just as important, if not more important. That's my take. You both made great contributions in different ways."

"Well, thanks, Dad; I appreciate that a lot, but you know I wish I was good enough to be competing out there. I cannot believe that at his age, and after all he's been through, Don is still good enough and able to run in these Games."

"It's quite remarkable," said Elizabeth Wells, "quite remarkable. He's as a strong as an ox, being able to run like this at his age. Now, tell me, I've forgotten. What event is he in?"

"The hurdles, Mum, the hurdles, just as he was in 1932 and 1936. I am still amazed. Here we are in 1948 and he is competing in his third Olympics, and with a long war in between."

"Pity about what the war did, for lots of reasons," said Wells senior. "You would have had your chance in 1940 and 1944. I know that you would have been selected and would have done well."

Jesse squeezed Roland's hand, not wishing to have his father's comment raise his inner anger over being deprived of both opportunities. His father's comment touched a raw nerve.

"No good crying over spilt milk," Roland responded in a soft voice.

Jesse gave him a beautiful smile, a way of saying "bygones will be bygones."

"Mum, have you read the program?"

"Oh, my gosh! You didn't tell us!"

"What are you talking about, Elizabeth?" said Frederick.

"It's the first part, dealing with the Opening Ceremony, right at the beginning, look who is saying the Olympic Oath...that's wonderful!"

"Wing Commander Donald Finlay, DFC, Royal Air Force," said Roland. "Don's saying the oath, isn't that just great?"

"Oh my," said Elizabeth. "What an occasion. The King and Queen will be so proud to have a Battle of Britain pilot saying the oath."

The Opening Ceremony began.

The moment came when Don Finlay stepped forward to swear the Olympic Oath on behalf of all the nations participating.

Wing Commander Finlay stood erect, and in a clear and powerful voice said in measured phrases these words:

"We swear that we will take part in the Olympic Games, in loyal competition, respecting the regulations which govern them, and desirous of participating in them, in the true spirit of sportsmanship, for the honor of our country, and for the glory of sport."

Wembley Stadium was awestruck. The words resonated.

Athens was restored in those words.

The Wells family swallowed. The whole stadium was electrified. The Opening Ceremony concluded and the 1948 London Olympic Games began.

In his final Olympics, the famous British war veteran ran in his event, the 110-meter hurdles. Don Finlay tripped on the last hurdle, and would have won another medal, but did not. However, together with Godfrey Rampling, Freddie Wolf, Godfrey Brown, and Bill Roberts their places were secure in the annals of Olympic history and the hearts and minds of the British people.

In Berlin in 1936, they had the first of many *Finest Hours*.

Chapter Twenty-One
FULL CIRCLE
OSBORNE HOUSE
ISLE OF WIGHT, HAMPSHIRE, ENGLAND
AUTUMN 1969

Queen Victoria loved Osborne House on the Isle of Wight like no other of her private residences, away from Buckingham Palace and the cares of state. She entertained Kaiser Wilhelm there, ensuring that his every need was met. On her passing, the great house and fine gardens passed into the care of the Royal Navy, first as a Naval College, the precursor to Britannia Royal Naval College, at Dartmouth in Devon, and later as the Navy's convalescent home for officers, a splendid place and quiet location for those recovering from war injuries.

By the 1960s there were few casualties of war to enter the fine portals of Osborne House, located conveniently just across the Solent from the Royal Naval Hospital at Haslar, in Gosport. The facilities had been much improved over the years since the war, with excellent physiotherapy and a retired surgeon rear admiral in overall charge. The officers' wardroom and food was nothing less than superb. Those who had been wounded in the Queen's service were well look after, indeed.

In the summer of 1969, one of the few active serving naval officers to be transferred to Osborne House from Haslar Naval Hospital was Lieutenant Anthony Wells, Royal Navy, son of Roland Wells and grandson of Frederick Wells. He had been severely injured and was in the hospital for several months before being transferred to Osborne House to convalesce.

While in Haslar Naval Hospital, Anthony Wells shared a sick berth with a distinguished World War II veteran, retired Royal Navy Commander Taffy Rodd, who during World War II had, amongst many of his courageous exploits, attacked the Bismarck from HMS Ark Royal, flying the famous Swordfish, launching an aerial torpedo at the Bismarck. Taffy Rodd joined Wells in his Haslar sick berth some time after Wells had been transferred to Haslar from else-where. The older retired commander and the young lieutenant struck up a lifelong friendship in the sick berth, Taffy Rodd having been very badly injured in an accident in Italy, and undoubtedly had his life saved when the British Naval Attaché in Italy arranged for him to be flown to Haslar and the care of Surgeon Captain Bruce Victor Jones, Royal Navy. Captain Jones was treating Wells, along with Surgeon Commander Fulford, who would later in life distinguish himself by becoming an honorary surgeon to Queen Elizabeth.

When Wells and Rodd were bundled up for the journey across the River Solent, the naval nursing sister in charge of their ward, Sister Ovens, and her nurses shed a few tears. Despite their injuries, they had cheered up the ward, and the surgeon admiral in charge of Haslar had never seen such a distinguished group of household names visit Taffy Rodd, including, for instance, Lord Beatty, the son of the famous World War I Admiral of the Fleet the Lord Beatty, who would visit Rodd regularly with several other luminaries.

When they departed with two Navy sick berth attendants to help them, Wells was still on crutches and Rodd was in a wheelchair. On arrival by boat in Cowes, Isle of Wight, the ancient Osborne House Rolls Royce was sent down to the pier by the retired surgeon admiral to greet them and transport them and their helpers to Osborne. This was the beginning of an auspicious and memorable two and a half months for the young Anthony Wells.

Rodd and Wells began to liven up Osborne House just as they had Sister Ovens' ward. To Wells' surprise, he was the only serving Royal Naval officer at Osborne House. The other patients were all retired officers, and nearly all were recovering like Taffy Rodd from non-service related injuries and illnesses acquired in retirement. Several were from the Army and Royal Air Force, since the Navy had opened up Osborne House to the other two services to help maximize the use of the fine facilities. Wells, as the only serving naval officer, was given the suite designed for Kaiser Wilhelm when he visited Queen Victoria at Osborne House. It included a sunken bath in the floor, with a rail, ideal for Wells to move in and out of the water, a therapy that he found most beneficial.

About three weeks into Wells' and Rodd's convalescence, it was made known by the staff that a retired Royal Air Force group captain would be joining the following day, and that he was in a wheelchair because he had become a paraplegic as a result of a tragic car accident. He could no longer walk. The staff wanted all present to be aware of the new patient's condition so as to be prepared to help him. It was also made known that he was spending his time moving between the three Services' convalescent homes, in order for him to have a change of location and more variety.

Anthony Wells was about to have a major surprise, one that despite the very sad circumstances of this person's situation, was to have a dramatic impact on him and several of the other patients, and particularly Taffy Rodd.

Anthony Wells' first meeting and greeting with the new patient has stayed with him always.

Group Captain Donald Finlay, DFC, Royal Air Force, retired, entered the company of Taffy Rodd and Anthony Wells.

"Dad, you will not believe this, but guess who arrived today at Osborne

House?"

Wells was calling his father, Roland, at his home near Coventry.

"I'm all ears."

"Don Finlay, your friend from way back that you've talked about so much. He's here, and I have to tell you, Dad, he's in a wheelchair—lost the use of his legs when his car hydroplaned in bad weather and he crashed. He's a paraplegic. He's all that you've ever said about him. He's just an incredible person."

"Oh, my God, I don't believe it. This is such sad news. I have to talk with him, Anthony; I haven't talked with him in years, it's so long since we communicated—must be when he retired from the RAF. I lost track of him. That's some years ago. He was thirty-eight years old in 1948 when he ran that last Olympic race. I shall never ever forget it, and he was leading and fell at the last hurdle. Does he know that you're my son?"

"Of course, Dad, I told him who I was once he settled in. I told him before dinner this evening. I thought I'd call you now so that I could talk with him over breakfast tomorrow, me and Taffy Rodd. They already get on like a house on fire. I am already waiting for these two World War II aviators to start their stories!"

"I bet, Anthony. Look, give him my best in the morning and find out a good time for me to call him, so that we can have a good private chat. I don't want to overload him if he's not up to it."

"Will do, Dad, I will chat with him over breakfast, promise."

Father and son chatted for another ten minutes or so, the older Wells recounting Don Finlay's exploits. His mother came on the line later; she, too, was greatly saddened to hear the bad news about Don Finlay's injuries. Jesse and Anthony chatted for some time, before his father clearly wanted to come back into the conversation.

His parting words were music in Anthony's ears.

"Your mother and I want to come down and visit you, in any case. We haven't seen you since our last visit to Haslar. Give Don my best, find a good time for me to chat with him, and I'll call. Think about the best time for us to visit, Anthony. Find out what the rules are about visitors, please."

After fond farewells, the Wells family ended their telephone call. The emotional impact was significant.

Anthony Wells realized as he climbed into the bed once slept in by Kaiser Wilhelm that he would have the honor and pleasure to spend time with Don Finlay, and also that he faced the very sensitive challenge to develop a relationship with a great athlete and war hero who was now crippled for life. He had to think through how best to approach this fine human being who was now a shadow of his former physical self.

In the days preceding Roland and Jesse Wells' arrival from Coventry, Anthony and Taffy befriended Don Finlay. He needed all the support that warmhearted people could provide. His paraplegia had taken an enormous toll on a man that had competed in three Olympic Games. Taffy Rodd was the most perfect medicine, a therapy that no doctor could prescribe. He listened, reminisced, joked, told wartime stories, recalled people, places, and great events past to which they both could relate—a perfect combination of antidotes to help Don Finlay find himself again, and reconnected with the person that he truly was, irrespective of his physical condition.

Over the ten days before his father and mother arrived, Anthony got to know Don Finlay the man, the inner spirit that had propelled him from boy aircraft apprentice to world class athlete, courageous pilot, and successful senior RAF officer. Wells constantly dwelt on the positive, drawing out Don Finlay in ways that only a young officer could, admiring and appreciating all that Finlay had achieved. They addressed each other as Don and Tony. Finlay insisted that Wells drop the 'Sir' after they first met. This was difficult for the Dartmouth trained Navy lieutenant, but it worked in the end. After several days of pushing Don around the grounds of Osborne house, stopping for prolonged chats, the two men became close friends.

"Don, may I make a suggestion please?"

"Of course, go ahead."

"Well, I've been thinking. Why don't you write a book, or books—you've got several in you. You have a great story to tell, an autobiography, together with lots of short stories, vignettes of all that has happened to you. It will make great reading. People will love to read your stories. How about it? Let's get you a typewriter."

"You're so much like your father, though I can see your mother in you, too. Your dad is one of the most positive and generous people I have ever known. You are a chip off the old block, Tony. That's not a bad idea. Let me think about it. I just don't want to live on memories right now."

"Don, it's not just memories, it's the now, the present, telling people like me and my generation about what you did so that we can all learn from you. You'd make a great lecturer—go on the lecture circuit."

"That may be fun." Finlay was motivated.

"Look, sir, sorry, Don, you will knock the socks off any lecture audience. I listened for three years to so-called lecturers droning on at Durham. You know the people that I always enjoyed were the World War II veterans, men who had fought in the war. I always remember volunteering for a dig at Housesteads on Hadrian's Wall, as cheap unpaid labor to help a guy called Birley, Professor Birley, unearth some great buried finds. Archeology was not my subject, but I could listen to Eric Birley all day—he entranced us with his descriptions of the Roman Army in Britain, and you know why, Don, because he was a World War II Army veteran, and worked in military intelligence in North Africa. He tied it all together. You do the same—enthrall the likes of me and my generation with your life and experiences."

"Tony. You're quite a talker yourself. Maybe I should listen to you! Let's get some coffee, and chat some more. I'm feeling cold."

The two of them moved on.

One of the prettiest nurses at Osborne House took quite a shine to Finlay, still a handsome man, attractive to any women of any age who could see the inner man, the real character. Wells deftly handed off to her his wheelchair pushing duty, confiding in her. He could see that she found Finlay a likable, attractive older man. He could also sense that she felt very sorry for him, knowing his past. However, pity was not her motivation, she liked Finlay for the man he was. The two of them struck up a relationship. She was soon to find out what had happened to Finlay in his private life.

When Jesse and Roland Wells arrived by ferry at Cowes, they were both looking forward so much to seeing their son again and also meeting Don Finlay after such a long interlude. They were also nervous, being unsure what to expect or how to react.

The first meeting put aside all worries. The natural friendship since the 1930s could not be eroded. It was as if the clock stood still, and the two men were back in their primes—athletes again, talking, joking, full of promise and aspirations for athletic prowess.

The day at Osborne House was memorable. They spent many hours reminiscing and bonding. Anthony listened with intense pleasure. He saw his father in a new light. His mother was radiant, uplifted by her husband's camaraderie with his friend, who though older than Roland, shared complete mutual respect, trust, and liking.

While Don went to his room to prepare for lunch, aided by his nurse, Roland confided privately with Jesse while Anthony chatted with Taffy Rodd.

"Jesse, I'm worried."

"I can see it, Roland, in spite of your brave face and smiles. Are we thinking the same thing?"

"I'm sure. He's depressed...seriously depressed. He confided in me."

"I agree. He's putting on a brave face, but he's down, really down, Roland. I feel for him. He's such a wonderful person."

"Well, while we were chatting privately and, by the way, thanks for taking Anthony and Taffy Rodd off so we could be alone and have some time together, he told me some pretty sad things."

"Like what?"

"Well, for starters, his wife left him after the accident—couldn't take it. They're divorced. He literally is a nomad, a retired RAF senior officer, moving from one convalescent home to another. Jesse, it's tragic. I am so worried about him."

"Did she run off with someone?"

"I didn't ask, he didn't tell, no point I thought in rubbing salt in an open wound."

"Very wise, Roland, what do you think we should do? We should invite him home. Let's ask him to stay with us for a few weeks. We've got so much spare room. We can take him down to Wales to stay with the Welsh relations."

Jesse was referring to Roland's other siblings, who had been farming in Wales since 1950. Roland's father had sold Coventry Gear in the late 1940s to a large British engineering company for a very tidy sum, and then bought a large mixed farm in south Warwickshire on the Oxfordshire border. His retirement life was to be farming. He soon tired of cattle and arable farming, and wanted to live in the mountains into his very old age. Frederick Wells bought several thousand acres of open sheep grazing land in central Wales, near the Élan Valley. He bought three farms and a hotel in addition. Roland stayed in Coventry, and his siblings took up sheep farming with their spouses and children, a complete change from the 'hurley-burley' of running a major industrial company in the heart of the Midlands. Frederick had given them all a choice. The large family home near Coventry was sold, and after the sojourn at Wolcott Manor, they all would move to central Wales, and lived there for the rest of their lives, with the exception of Roland and Jesse, and their children.

"That's a great idea. He will love the mountain air. My mother can fix him up a very nice ground floor suite so that he has easy wheelchair access, and he can sit and enjoy the bar life at the Red Lion. He can write, like Anthony has suggested. My sister Betty can help him find publishers."

"Now we're talking, Roland. Let's just not overwhelm him; otherwise, he may think we're trying to take over his life. Let's be gentle."

"I'll leave it to you. You're better at this sort of thing than me. He'll listen to you more then me on this subject."

"Let's chat then over lunch."

"Good idea."

Lunch and the rest of the afternoon went well. The precious hours that they all spent together were magical.

As Roland and Jesse prepared to leave and take a taxi down to the ferry, they confirmed with Don the plans for his various visits in the New Year of 1970. Don's old friend and his wife had become, not just reunited in a few short hours; they were now firmly installed as a support group.

The farewell was tough. Jesse held back her tears. Taffy was now out of his wheelchair and using a walking stick, and Anthony was off his crutches and was using a stick, too. Intense daily physiotherapy and exercise were strengthening Wells, and his Navy PT instructor was getting him back into shape after months of muscle atrophy. Anthony and Taffy were all smiles. Don was pushed by his favorite nurse. Jesse gave him a tender kiss on the cheek. Roland shook hands with Don, stressing that they looked forward to seeing him in the spring, once Don's winter stay at the RAF Convalescent Home was over in March 1970. They would call regularly and write. Roland smiled, "Can't wait to read your first book, Don, it's going to be a winner, just like its author."

They all waved as the taxi drove down the driveway of Osborne House. Jesse and Roland planned to spend the night in Southsea, just across the Solent adjacent to Portsmouth and the great Royal Naval Base, with Jesse's late brother John's widow and her new husband. As the ferry pulled away for the ride to Portsmouth, both Jesse and Roland were overcome with emotion, so very grateful that their son was on the mend and going back to the Navy and a new and exciting appointment, but at the same time, full of foreboding about Don's mental state and his clear depression.

"I chatted with Taffy privately about Don. He's going to talk with the Surgeon Rear Admiral, to see what they can do to help Don get out of the doldrums."

"Oh, good, that will help a lot. He needs all the love and care that he can get. I feel so sorry for him, Roland."

The ferry pulled alongside, and they made the short walk to where they had parked their car. They headed to Southsea and Jesse's brother's widow's house. For a few hours, they would have other things to occupy their hearts and minds.

Four months later, Lieutenant Wells was at sea. It was April 1970. A Royal Air Force Shackleton martime patrol aircraft circled the ship, preparing to drop mail via a special floating container, a well used procedure, and one that always linked the Royal Navy and the RAF in unquestionable camaraderie. The drop was perfect, and the RAF pilot flew over the top of the ship at very low altitude as it left the area. The ship's boat quickly retrieved the container.

Wells was standing on the port bridge wing during the first dog watch later in the day, the first chance that he'd had to look at his mail.

The distinctive Coventry postmark and his father's fine copperplate hand-writing told Wells instantly that his father's letter would be the first to be opened.

As he opened up the larger than normal envelope, some newspaper cuttings fell onto the deck and he quickly retrieved them in case the wind took them along the port waist and over the side.

Lieutenant Wells was overcome. He just stared into the ocean, and lifted his head skyward.

A chief petty officer came to his side.

"Are you all right, sir? Is everything okay? Not bad news, I hope. The mail sometimes brings bad news, as well as good news. No *Dear John* letters I hope, sir, from the girlfriend back in Pompey?"

"I'm fine, thank you. I'm fine. Some bad news, but no *Dear John* letter—a little worse, in fact."

"I'm sorry, sir; I'll leave you in peace."

The newspaper cuttings were obituaries from the leading British newspapers. Don Finlay had died on April 18, 1970.

Anthony read his dad's long letter and the note from his mother several times, his mind whirling back to Osborne House and the last farewell with Don Finlay and Taffy Rodd. As he pictured the two of them waving to him as the Rolls Royce took Lieutenant Wells from Osborne House down to the pier in Cowes and back to the Royal Navy, tears welled inside him. He thought back to his last night at Osborne, the memorable trip from the House to the Medway Queen moored in the Medina River, and a farewell party, with special arrange-ments with the Medway Queen staff to provide a gangway to take Don's wheel-chair. It was a wonderful evening, full of hope and good cheer. Despite their ages, Wells had mused, the future was still theirs, these incredible men who had helped save the world. It was not to be for Don Finlay.

A gentle hand touched Wells' shoulder. His commanding officer was at his side.

"Are you okay, Tony? You haven't had some bad news, have you?"

"Yes, sir, a little."

His commanding officer could see the obituaries of Don Finlay in Wells' hand.

"I'm sorry, Tony. I'll leave you alone."

"It's okay, sir; he would want me to do just what he would do. Carry on."

His commanding officer let him be.

Anthony Wells secured the letters and cuttings, placed them in his pocket, stood straight, faced aft, and saluted the White Ensign flying from the main mast, a final salute to the memory of Group Captain Donald Finlay, DFC, Royal Air Force.

Epilogue

Most of the leading characters in this story lived long and mainly happy lives after the conclusion of World War II and the 1948 Olympic Games.

Air Chief Marshal Sir Keith Park died in 1975, at age 82, in New Zealand, the country of his birth, where the author did extensive research in the Auckland War Memorial Museum on Park's life. After command of Eleven Group in 1940, Park was later appointed to be the air officer commanding Malta in 1942, saving Malta and contributing significantly to the Allied victory in the Mediterranean, the precursor major campaign to the D-Day landings. In 1944, he was appointed the air officer commander-in-chief Middle East command, and in February 1945, he was made the allied air commander Southeast Asia. He was promoted to air chief marshal on December 20, 1945. Park secured, on his retirement, a Vickers Supermarine Spitfire for display in Auckland. He held several distinguished positions in New Zealand after retiring from the Royal Air Force. Although a distinctively loyal and gracious person, Keith Park could never quite forgive how the 'British Establishment' treated Air Chief Marshal Dowding on the conclusion of the Battle of Britain. Lord Tedder's comments recorded in the Dedication of this book and the statue erected in London to mark Keith Park's enormous contribution to Allied victory in World War II have set the record straight for all time. Keith Park is up there with General George Patton, Field Marshal Sir Bernard Montgomery, Fleet Admiral Chester Nimitz, Marshal Zhukov, and Field Marshal Sir William Slim as one of the all time great commanders of modern times.

Jesse Owens' life ebbed and flowed after World War II, with several perturbations. He had financial problems, never quite stabilizing his personal life because of the inherent prejudice for blacks that still pervaded the United States way into the 1960s. However, to Owens' great pleasure, President Dwight Eisenhower reestablished Owens as a true national hero in 1955, when he appointed him United States Ambassador of Sports. In 1976, President Ford conferred on him the Presidential Medal of Freedom, the United States' highest civilian award. Jesse Owens had been a smoker for thirty-five years, and eventually contracted lung cancer. He died in 1980 in Tucson, Arizona, at age 66. On March 28, 1990, President George Herbert Walker Bush awarded Jesse Owens posthumously the Congressional Gold Medal, an award that placed Jesse Owens forever as the United States' premier athlete. He is buried in Oakwoods Cemetery in Chicago, Illinois.

The only one of the story's characters to see the new millennium and live to be over one hundred was the gold medal winner Godfrey Rampling. He died on June 20, 2009, aged 101, mourned by his daughter, the famous actress Charlotte Rampling. Rampling was regarded by the whole British athletic community as the greatest relay runner of all time. His lap in 1936 in Berlin will stand forever as one of the greatest races ever, joining him and Jesse Owens in an inseparable bond.

Don Finlay's later years have been described in the final chapter of this book, but suffice it to say that Finlay was never quite given the honors and recognition that, for example, were conferred on Harold Abrahams. Although he never won Olympic Gold, his performance in three Olympic Games and the British Empire Games was outstanding. Although clearly not an officer-politician, Finlay's RAF career was extraordinarily distinguished. He may not have been senior staff officer material in the new post-war Ministry of Defense, but he was a true leader and highly capable senior officer. He never received the official recognition from the 'British Establishment' that was his due. The life and times of Don Finlay should undoubtedly be the subject of much more public recognition via all forms of modern media. He is a true legend in his own right.

Frederick Wells died of cancer, he, too, a smoker. He is buried very near to Llandrindod Wells in Powys in a beautiful ancient country churchyard overlooking the Welsh mountains that he came to love after closing the industrial and wartime chapters of his life. His wife and several other family members, including two of his children, are buried beside him. He lived a long and fruitful life, and gave much to charity, mainly though the Freemasons, of which he was a loyal member for all of his adult life. He passed on to his grandchildren and great grandchildren his inventiveness, entrepreneurial skill and energy, and dedication to doing the right thing. The church was packed to overflowing and beyond when he and his wife Elizabeth died, she passing away some years after Frederick.

Admiral Canaris was tortured by the SS, and executed on April 9, 1945, just a short while before the German surrender. His life and work for British intelligence must be the subject of much further research and his role recognized more fully in supporting the Allied cause behind the Nazi lines, one of the all time great espionage stories of history.

John Cecil Masterman became a distinguished Oxford don. He died in 1977.

Sir Harry Hinsley became a Cambridge don, a professor and vice chancellor of Cambridge University, and the official historian of the *History of British Intelligence in World War II* in several volumes. He was successfully a Fellow and Master of St. John's College Cambridge, where he had been an undergraduate in 1939, leaving the college on recruitment to the highly secretive Bletchley Park. He was chairman of the author's Ph.D. board, and his mentor. The existence of Enigma and Ultra was not released by the British government until 1974. Harry Hinsley died in 1998, aged 79.

Both Roland and Jesse Wells were inveterate smokers and both died from the effects of smoking. They are buried in St. Thomas' churchyard in Keresley, near Coventry, together with many family members. They lived long and happy lives—a relationship and marriage that were sustained during the best of times and the worst of times. Their son is the author of this book. Their lives epitomize the 'Greatest Generation.' Born into a world that witnessed the horrors of World War I, they lived through the 'Great Depression,' and the gathering storms of the 1930s as World War II approached. They lived through the darkest days of World War II, and played their roles in the final triumphant victory. In peace, they contributed to the rebuilding process and doing good works. Their courage and fortitude stand out today like beacons, together with all the other lead characters in this book, people who lived through times the likes of which the world will hopefully never see again.

The recent financial crisis, the continuing threat from terrorism, Mid East dissension and revolt, a possible epic clash of cultures as Moslem Sunnis and Shiites collide, the threat of a nuclear Iran, and an emerging powerful China, must be seen in the context of the life and times of these people. We can learn so much from their example—their courage and fortitude in never giving up, never giving way to the line of least resistance, and having faith in their values, their country, and fellow human beings. We can all reclaim, in modern form, the heritage and enduring strength that they passed on.

CPSIA information can be obtained
at www.ICGtesting.com
Printed in the USA
BVHW041257221221
624694BV00011B/258